ATHENIAN
DEMOCRACY

Frank M. Covey, Jr.,
Loyola Lectures in Political Analysis
Thomas S. Engeman
General Editor

Our late colleague Richard S. Hartigan founded the Frank M. Covey, Jr., Lectures in Political Analysis to provide a continuing forum for the reanimation of political philosophy. The lectures are not narrowly constrained by a single topic nor do they favor a particular perspective. Their sole aim is to foster serious theoretical inquiry, with the expectation that this effort will contribute in essential ways to both human knowledge and political justice.

Athenian Democracy

MODERN MYTHMAKERS
AND
ANCIENT THEORISTS

Arlene W. Saxonhouse

University of Notre Dame Press
NOTRE DAME AND LONDON

© 1996 by
University of Notre Dame Press
Notre Dame, Indiana 46556
All Rights Reserved

Manufactured in the United States of America

Book design by Wendy Torrey and Jeannette Morgenroth
Set in 12/14 Centaur by Books International
Printed and bound by Thomson-Shore, Inc.

Library of Congress Cataloging-in-Publication Data

Saxonhouse, Arlene W.
    Athenian democracy : modern mythmakers and
ancient theorists / Arlene W. Saxonhouse.
        p.   cm. — (Frank M. Covey, Jr. Loyola lectures
in political analysis)
    Includes bibliographical references and index.
    ISBN 0-268-00650-4 (alk. paper)
        1. Democracy—Greece—History.   2. Democracy—
Greece—Athens—History.   I. Title.   II. Series.
JC75.D36S39   1996
320.438'5—dc20   95-47268
                                                            CIP

∞ *The paper used in this publication meets the minimum
requirements of the American National Standard for Information Sciences—
Permanence of Paper for Printed Library Materials,
ANSI Z39.48-1984*

For my mother,
Olly Warmbrunn

It is my sad privilege to be the presenter of the last Frank M. Covey Lectures organized by Richard Hartigan. I did not know Dick well. Our contacts were primarily arranging for this series of lectures, but his warmth, encouragement, and enthusiam were responsible for my presenting the lectures on which this book is based. I deeply regret that I am not able to repay that encouragement directly to him.

A. W. S.

Contents

Preface

But so different was the style of society then and with those people, from what it is now and with us, that I think little edification can be obtained from their writings on the subject of government.... The introduction of this principle of representative democracy has rendered useless almost everything written before on the structure of government; and, in great measure, relieves our regret, if the political writings of Aristotle, or of any other ancient, have been lost, or are unfaithfully rendered or explained to us.

Thomas Jefferson, Letter to Isaac Tiffany, 1816[1]

My intent in this volume is to reject Jefferson's claim, not by asking that we model ourselves on the practice of ancient democracy, but that we learn from the ancient authors who experienced that practice: the contradictions, the tensions, the possibilities, the benefits of that complex form of government. An alternative title for this work might have been "The Use and Abuse of Ancient History" to suggest how visions of ancient Athens have served to support or undermine political visions of the wished-for political community.[2]

Let me express my gratitude to those who invited me to give the lectures and who provided the opportunity to develop inchoate reflections into a series of lectures and then into a book. I thank also those who attended the lectures and asked the questions that led, in part, to the delay in completing the book. The questions needed to be addressed and I hope that those who queried me recognize my attempts to take seriously their concerns in the present volume. I am especially grateful to the members of the Political Science Department at Loyola University for hosting me during the week of the lectures and most especially to Thomas Engeman for his hospitality, his concern that my every need was met, and his encouragement to finish the promised book which took much longer than it should have to complete.

I also would like to thank the Office of the Vice-President for Research at the University of Michigan, which provided funds to help me through the final stages of producing this volume. Eric Kos was a model research assistant, always eager, willing, enthusiastic, and able. He did far more than was expected throughout. To my husband, Gary, thanks once again for the gentle prodding that keeps me going and the love that puts all into perspective.

Ann Arbor, 1995

ATHENIAN
DEMOCRACY

CHAPTER I

The Mythmakers

"A TYRANNY IN THE HANDS OF THE PEOPLE": that was the democratic regime established by Solon—or so pronounced the eighteenth-century historian William Mitford (1838, 4:10). "In their rational and secular approach, in their commitment to political freedom and individual autonomy in a constitutional, republican and democratic public life, the Athenians of Pericles' day are closer to the values of our era than any culture that has appeared since antiquity. That is why Periclean Athens has such a powerful meaning for us" (Kagan 1991, 10). So writes a distinguished contemporary scholar of ancient Athens. Athens, the first democratic regime, has been a symbol of what is dangerous, of what is glorious, of the threats of mob rule, of the individual as free, of the chaos of greed, of the beauty of devotion to the city. As a symbol, Athens has played a variety of roles in modern ideologies, but this has often meant that too little attention has been paid to the way in which the ancient Athenians thinkers understood their democracy, the challenges it raised for those experiencing it, and the theoretical questions it forced them to confront. The history of ancient democracy in the last three centuries has been one of use and abuse. The ancient Athenian authors whom I discuss in the following chapters, living in that democracy, needed neither to use nor abuse it, but to understand it and to grapple with its principles.[1]

I

Early in his intellectual career, the preeminent English philosopher of the seventeenth century, Thomas Hobbes, translated the writings of Thucydides. In the prefatory remarks to his translation Hobbes makes clear his own distaste for the democratic regime of fifth-century Athens. Thucydides was, in Hobbes's words:

> sufficiently qualified to have become a great demagogue, and of great authority with the people. But it seemeth he had no desire at all to meddle in the government: because in those days it was impossible for any man to give good and profitable counsel for the commonwealth, and not incur the displeasure of the people. For their opinion was such of their own power, and of the facility of achieving whatsoever action they undertook, that such men only swayed the assemblies, and were esteemed wise and good commonwealth's men, as did put them upon the most dangerous and desperate enterprises. Whereas he that gave them temperate and discreet advice, was thought a coward. (1975, 12–13)

No sentimental attachment to democracy influenced Hobbes's analysis of Thucydides' work: "For his opinion touching the government of the state," Hobbes writes about Thucydides, "it is manifest that he least of all liked the democracy," adding a few lines later: "He praiseth the government of Athens, when it was mixed of *the few* and *the many*; but more he commendeth it, both when Peisistratus reigned, (saving that it was an usurped power), and when in the beginning of this war it was democratical in name, but in effect monarchical under Pericles" (1975, 13–14). For Hobbes, Thucydides' hostility to democracy was in part what made him worthy of translation.

In the actual translation, when he comes to Pericles' famous Funeral Oration, Hobbes uses the following words to turn Thucydides' Greek into English: "We have a form of government, not fetched by imitation from the laws of our neighbouring states; (nay, we are rather a pattern to others, than they to us); which, because in the administration it hath respect not to a few, but to the multitude, is called a democracy" (1975, 131–32). Many have been the translations into English both in England and in America since Hobbes's 1628 translation. The one most frequently used today is Rex Warner's translation in the Penguin edition. The passage just quoted from Hobbes's translation of Pericles' Funeral Oration appears in Warner as: "Let me say that our system of government does not copy the institutions of our neighbours. It is more the case of our being a model to others, than of our imitating anyone else. Our constitution is called a democracy *because power is in the hands not of a minority but of the whole people*" (Thucydides 1954, 117).[2] Generations of contemporary students have been brought up on Warner's translation, but we should note the difference in translation between the two: one translator, Hobbes, clearly opposes democracy, the other, Warner, is sympathetic to it. It is the former, Hobbes, who is more accurate. There is nothing in the language of Pericles' speech as presented by Thucydides that suggests that *dēmokratia* entails power in the hands of "the whole people." It is, rather, as Hobbes had translated, "administration [with] respect not to a few, but to the multitude."[3]

Warner's mistranslation does suggest, however, the confusion that surrounds our understanding of Athenian democracy, not at all a surprising state of affairs since the term, for all its emotive and normative power, hardly enjoys a precise and universally accepted definition today. Consent, participation, equality, rights, liberties, self-determination, and autonomy all mingle unclearly in our understanding of democracy, as we now accuse some countries and some leaders of being antidemocratic and praise others as being or becoming democratic. This is not the place to try to offer a clear definition of democracy for our, or for the ancient, world, but Warner's mistranslation alerts us to the problems of imposing our own expectations of democratic systems, specifically as participatory, as translating the will of the people into public policy, on the ancient Athenians. To do so may give us false expectations about the possibilities of a democratic polity, while the romantic view of ancient democracy that has taken hold since Hobbes's translation (but is now being questioned by some contemporary historians) has hindered our ability to grasp the significance of that regime.

II

The study of the institutions of ancient democracy has experienced a major resurgence among scholars in the last decade as the methods and language of social science are joined to the study of ancient history and archaeology (Ober 1989a; Manville 1990; Strauss 1986); careful measurement and epigraphy are all exploited in attempts to calculate exactly how democracy functioned in Athens. No longer simply satisfied with the description of Athenian institutions as they appear in *Athenian Constitution*, historians of the classical world, in language reminiscent of the behavioral revolution in political science of some decades ago, now ask who attended the assembly, who filled the law courts, and how many citizens actually participated. They ask how important was the assembly which passed decrees, in contrast to the juries which passed judgment on those who proposed decrees. "[W]e must go beyond constitutional history to a study of the ways in which individuals combine to influence the policies of their city," claims W. R. Connor (1971, 5). Such scholars now write of mass and elite, of center and periphery, of localism, of apathy.

In one of the classic books about Athenian democracy, called simply *Athenian Democracy* and published in 1957 with a 1964 reprint, the classical scholar A. H. M. Jones claims: "Prima Facie the Athenian Democracy would seem to have been a perfectly designed machine for expressing and putting into effect the will of the people" ([1957] 1964, 3). In a similar vein, the Marxist scholar G. E. M. de Ste. Croix has effused: "Even many Classical scholars have failed to realise the extraordinary originality of Greek democracy, which, in the fundamental sense of *taking political decisions by majority vote of all citizens*, occurred earlier than in any other society we know about" (1981, 284). Though more recent historians have been busy questioning the adequacy of this rosy picture of the political life of Athenian democracy, one that could have existed without slaves and without empire according to Jones, the discussion has still been carried on primarily in terms of the "will of the sovereign people" and whether the machine of Athenian politics could transform that "will" into practice. Thus, we find among the writings of our contemporary historians the painstakingly detailed studies of M. H. Hansen, who calculates how many Athenians could really have attended the assembly at any point in time by measuring how much space a seated adult male occupied and thereby calculates the seating capacity of the Pnyx; he concludes that it could have been no more than one-seventh of the potential voters in the fifth century and between one-third and one-fourth in the fourth century; and that is the maximum (1983, 16–17). De Ste. Croix's "majority vote of all citizens" may have been an impossible goal. Hansen is not alone in raising questions about the number of attendees at the assemblies. R. K. Sinclair, for one, thinks that attendance must have been considerably below the 6,000 or so who could fit into the Pnyx at one time, especially in the fourth century when the increase in the pay for attendance at the assembly "indicates continuing difficulties in securing support for the assembly" (1988,

119). And another author, L. B. Carter, has recently concluded: "The Athenians had *never seen* a full meeting of the citizen body, though," he claims, somewhat surprisingly to my mind, "the very idea of democracy was predicated on it." Importing the modern idea of representation back to ancient Athens, he argues: "From the very start they must have accepted that any meeting of the assembly was bound to be a sample of the citizenship—and not even a random sample" (1986, 193).[4]

Other historians have been concerned not so much with how many but who attended: Was it the poor rather than the rich as Carter suggests in his book? Did the wealthy, withdrawing from political life, let it be ruled by the nonwealthy; or, again, did the wealthy who had the resources to spend considerable leisure time at the assembly involve themselves? Or as Josiah Ober argues (1989a, 134–35), was it the case that the wealthy could not have dominated because demographically they were a small percentage of the population? The debate of late has raged among these historians about whether the *ecclēsia* or assembly could have incorporated, or in more modern language "represented," all the elements of the citizen body.[5] And once the citizens were collected together (whatever percentage of the citizen population they were), who spoke and who proposed the up to 400 proposals each year? Hansen questions further, as rightly he should—and as we all should have—how votes were actually taken. Without computerized voting, how do you calculate a closely divided vote when there are 6,000 people sitting in the assembly? There are references in the Greek to the raising of hands, but who counts? Others, such as Raphael Sealey (1987) and Martin Ostwald (1986), have tried to rescue the reputation of Athens by transforming her from a democracy, meaning by that term the rule of a disorderly assembly, to a republic governed by the rule of courts and the law.

My concern is that all such historical analyses, while raising important questions about any vision of Athenian "direct democracy" in terms of a New England town meeting or as a "face-to-face" society (Finley 1973, 17), still bring to the study of ancient democracy our conceptions of democracy as it has emerged in the nineteenth and into the twentieth centuries. Thus, scholars are asking how sovereign were the people, to what degree did they or did they not participate, were they informed, were the voters representative, how were votes counted, were the courts a brake on or subject to the assembly, as if these were the questions the Athenians asked about their own political regime. We, living in twentieth-century democracies and seeing new ones emerging almost daily, too often begin our analyses of Athenian democracy by assuming "a people" whose "will" must be transformed through popular participation in the assembly into public policy, with the question of participation at the heart of our concerns. For this view of democracy we must, I believe, thank Rousseau, who in his struggle to preserve both equality and freedom gave to modern discourse the language of the general will in its political context. Rousseau indeed weighs heavily on our understanding of ancient democracy—as seen in the passage quoted above from A. H. M. Jones—but the ancients lived in a period before the concept of will and popular sovereignty became the coin of political discourse. This was not the language with which they described their regime or thought about their political principles.[6]

III

We today are plagued in our study of ancient democracy by the lack of any author from Athens whom we might legitimately name a democratic theorist. No Rousseau, no Jefferson, no Mill populated the Athenian theoretical landscape. We can find occasional references in the plays praising democracy but no developed arguments for or explanations of it. In Aeschylus' *Persians*, for example, the Persian queen asks who is the shepherd of the people against whom the Persians have gone to war. The chorus responds in an oft-quoted phrase: "They are called slaves of no man, not listening to any one person" (241–42). In Aeschylus' *Suppliant Women*, the Argive monarch sets himself up as one who must listen to his people. To the suppliants seeking protection in Argos, he says: "Do not choose me as a judge. I said before, not without the *dēmos* would I do those things" (397–99).[7] Or in Euripides' *Suppliant Women* Theseus speaks of having set free the city "of equal votes" (353) and needing to persuade them when he goes among the *plēthos* of the city (*astos*) (355). In reply to the Theban herald asking for the "tyrant" of the city, he says that the herald has asked the wrong question, since "the city is free" and no one man rules; the people rule in turn, the poor equally with the rich (400–409). As a further defense he points to the equal access to justice of the rich and the weak (430–40). Haemon, in Sophocles' *Antigone*, lamely urges his father, Creon, to listen to the speech of the people of the city, to which Creon responds with anger: "Do you say that the city must tell me how to rule?" (734). Apart from the speeches of Euripides' Theseus, these are for the most part quick phrases that do not take us very far into the theoretical underpinnings of democracy, while Theseus' argument focuses primarily on the arbitrariness of the rule of the tyrant but does not offer a defense of the principle of equal participation.

Protagoras' speech in Plato's dialogue of the same name is perhaps the most sustained discourse in defense of democratic institutions that we have from Athens,[8] but this speech is set within a dialogue where Protagoras as the exponent of democratic principles of equality is made to look like a pompous fool. Protagoras' defense of democracy, nevertheless, is an important one and certainly the most theoretically sophisticated before Aristotle.

Protagoras begins by telling the story of Epimetheus (Hindsight) who lacks the foresight of his brother Prometheus. Epimetheus, assigned by Zeus to distribute the powers (*dunameis*) to each species as was fitting, distributes them all, tough skin, hooves, speed, etc., before he turns to men. All the powers have been used up and Epimetheus must go to his brother Prometheus, who gives men fire, and to Zeus, who gives them the two skills they need to live in cities: a sense of justice and a sense of shame. These are distributed equally among all men—unlike skills in flute playing or house building. Thus, Protagoras claims: "The Athenians and others . . . whenever they come together in counsel . . . appropriately listen to every man's opinion since it is fitting for each man to partake of this virtue or there would not be cities" (322d–323a). Since all share in the virtues that are necessary if cities are to exist, all will participate equally in the deliberations about the policies of the city. The democracy resides in the city's dependence on each man's sense of justice and of shame, qualities they all equally share. Of course, Socrates must come in and question what exactly these virtues necessary to politics are and whether they are one or many—and by the end he has Protagoras agreeing that excellence must be knowledge, which in turn must be taught and thus does not belong to us by nature or as a gift of Zeus; nor, finally, can it be in all men who will participate equally in a democratic regime. So much for equality and democracy in the *Protagoras*.

Thus, even in the most developed exposition of a justification for democracy, rather than in the dramatist's exhortation or simple expression of pride in the demos as ruler, we find reservations expressed and the direction of thought moving back to the leadership of the one who knows rather than to the whole population as political actors. The literary sources from the 150 to 200 years of democracy at Athens display, at best, an ambivalence about the value of a political system that allows the many to rule in their own self-interest. And yet ancient democracy at least for the last 150 years (perhaps because we do know so little about it) has become the shield behind which we have often come to place our own values. It has served as a model with which to stir up democratic patriotism; it has been used to flagellate modern, individualistic, liberal society, where we sit isolated in our focus on our private lives; and it has raised questions about the social science that supports such a society.

One of the first books that I was assigned when I was in graduate school was R. G. Collingwood's *An Autobiography*. Since the course was on the history of political thought and traveled only from the Greeks to Machiavelli, I was puzzled by the assignment of an autobiography of an English Idealist from the early twentieth century. Not surprisingly, there was reason in what seemed to a fresh B. A. as madness and that work has guided me since. The most important passage for me, one which I quote often, is the section in which Collingwood describes his intellectual confrontation with the Albert Memorial in London. Let me quote it here at some length:

> A year or two after the outbreak of war, I was living in London and working with a section of the Admiralty Intelligence Division in the rooms of the Royal Geographic Society. Every day I walked across Kensington Gardens and past the Albert Memorial. The Albert Memorial began by degrees to obsess me. . . . Everything about it was visibly mis-shapen, corrupt, crawling, verminous; for a time I could not bear to look at it, and passed with averted eyes; recovering from this weakness, I forced myself to look, and to face day by day the question: a thing so obviously, so incontrovertibly, so indefensibly bad, why had Scott done it? . . . What relation was there, I began to ask myself, between what he had done and what he had tried to do? Had he tried to produce a beautiful thing? . . . If so, he had of course failed. But had he perhaps been trying to produce something different? . . . If I found the monument merely loathsome, was that perhaps my fault? Was I looking in it for qualities it did not possess, and either ignoring or despising those it did? (1939, 29–30)

While we are hardly obsessed by the ugliness of the Greek world, we may be guilty, as Collingwood was with his Albert Memorial, of "looking in it for qualities it did not possess, and either ignoring or despising those it did."

For the rest of this chapter, let me rehearse how those looking to ancient democracy for "qualities it did not possess" have become mythmakers of Athenian democracy, using that political regime as a model either to be emulated or excoriated. These are authors, scholars, philosophers, politicians, pundits who were and are perhaps less interested in what ancient democracy was than in how it could be used for rhetorical and exhortatory purposes.[9] The mythmakers whom I shall discuss come from the England and America of the last 300 years or so; and in their adoration or abhorrence of ancient Athens have created barriers, I believe, to our ability to assess the lessons that ancient historians and philosophers drew from Athenian democracy. They have come to influence profoundly the ways in which ancient democracy has become part of the popular imagination. The ancient historians and philosophers, to whom I turn in the subsequent chapters, take us beyond the practice of democracy in ancient Athens and beyond a simplistic view of democracy as power in the hands of the whole people to a deeper sense of what democracy entails, its benefits, its defects, and especially its internal contradictions. Eschewing any uniform, coherent model of ancient democracy, they draw on democracy's multifaceted nature and force us to explore the underlying assumptions that characterize most regimes we might call democratic.

IV

In the heart of the rust belt in southeast Michigan is a town named Ypsilanti. Founded as a trading post in 1823 by Benjamin Woodruff and settlers from Ohio, Ypsilanti was originally known by the rather unoriginal name of Waterville. In 1833, however, the inhabitants agreed to change the name to Ypsilanti to honor Demetrius Ypsilanti, a general who commanded the Greek forces against the Turks during the Greek war of liberation. At the time, the inhabitants of what was then Waterville had no particular ties to Greece; Waterville was not filled with immigrants from Greece fondly recalling their homeland. They had all recently come from Ohio. The city was, however, filled with citizens eager to remind themselves of the Greek spirit that overthrew tyrants and founded the political model of self-rule. Ypsilanti is hardly the only city in the mid-1800s to be named or renamed with a view towards recalling the democratic regime and democratic spirit of ancient Athens. For the same reason Doric columns grace many an American front porch and bank facade. The Roman Republic with its aristocratic model of virtuous leaders and antimonarchical principles held sway over the thinking of the early years of the American Republic, but the more democratic, more participatory, vision of ancient Athens began weaving itself into the political consciousness of Americans in the 1820s.

We must remember that it was only with the French Revolution that the word "democracy" changes from a term laden with negative implications to a term of praise. Even those whom we might today call democratic theorists, such as Rousseau, thought that a democratic regime—and he was envisioning direct democracy—was neither desirable nor practical. Democracy was only possible among gods. At our own founding, Alexander Hamilton warns in *The Federalist*, No. 9: "It is impossible to read the history of the petty republics of Greece and Italy without feeling sensations of horror and disgust at the distractions with which they are continually agitated, and at the rapid succession of revolutions by which they were kept in a state of perpetual vibration between the extremes of tyranny and anarchy." The classic article on the use of democracy in the late eighteenth century by R.R. Palmer argues that even the word "democrat" does not appear in England or in France before 1784 and then speculates that it was the conservatives who used the term to denigrate their opponents. It is Palmer who notes that Burke calls "a perfect democracy" "the most shameless thing in the world." When "democrat" did appear without the derogatory overtones, Palmer adds, "[i]t remained generally a cold and even intellectual word" (1953, 212).

In the United States in the eighteenth century, the term "democracy" finds some favor in the writings of Thomas Paine—a far more radical writer than the authors of *The Federalist Papers*. Despite Madison's and Hamilton's warnings about ancient mobs and ancient chaos, Paine praises the democracy practiced by the Athenians:

> Though the ancient governments present to us a miserable picture of the condition of man, there is one which above all others exempts itself from the general description. I mean the democracy of the Athenians. We see more to admire and less to condemn, in that great, extraordinary people, than in anything which history affords. (1989, 167)

What makes Athenian democracy so admirable according to Paine is that it is not based on the principle of inheritance: "Kings succeed each other, not as rationals, but as animals," he says (1989, 163). The only problem posed by the model of ancient democracy is its size, a problem easily resolved by representation. While Hamilton and Madison found in representation the mechanism to control faction, "to refine and enlarge the public views by passing them through the medium of a chosen body of citizens" (*Federalist*, No. 10), in other words, a mechanism to tame the democratic vision of ancient democracy, Paine views representation only in terms of allowing democratic America to increase in size. "What Athens was in miniature, America will be in magnitude. The one was the wonder of the ancient world—the other is becoming the admiration and model of the present" (1989, 170).

Paine's admiration for the democracy of the Athenians was not, however, picked up by others; it was the Roman Republic that dominated political language and images. Thomas Gordon, for example, urged that the Roman Republic be the "standard and Pattern . . . , an Example to us" (quoted in Reinhold 1984, 96); John Adams, ignoring the profound differences between Rome and Athens, turned Athens into a "republican power" along with Rome as doing "more honor to our species than all the rest of it" (quoted in Reinhold 1984, 97).[10] Or, if they did not turn to the Roman Republic, the leaders of the newly emerging nation turned to Sparta, not Athens, which was "suspect because of its turbulent history, direct democracy, factionalism, and demagogues" (Reinhold 1984, 97). Sparta was celebrated for its free, virtuous, long-lived regime.[11] The democratic institutions of Athens were not the object of emulation. Palmer maintains that after 1800 the term "democracy" "went out of American popular usage . . . not to be revived until the founding of the Democratic party" (1953, 225).

I have been unable to ascertain whether the choice of the name for the new Democratic party that came into being in the late 1820s with Andrew Jackson at its helm had anything to do with a desire to recall the world of ancient Athens, but during the decade of the 1820s Americans began to turn to Greece rather than Rome, to Athenian democracy rather than Spartan discipline, as their model. The revolution in Greece in the early 1820s, the same revolution that led to the renaming of Waterville, Michigan, to Ypsilanti, evoked an emotional response that brought ancient Greek history and Athenian democracy to the center of the American consciousness. Numerous scholars write of a "Greek fever" spreading across America. Greek comes to replace Latin as *the* classical language and Edward Everett, a president of Harvard, a senator from Massachusetts, a secretary of state, becomes known for his great oratorical skills built on reminding audiences of the beauty of Greek culture.[12] The Greek rebels appealed via the philhellenes to the American people for help in 1822 and 1823, and we find local groups supporting the rebellion and collecting money to help the Greeks free themselves from the tyrannical Turks as Americans now identified Athens as the birthplace of their democracy.

Here, for example, is the great orator Daniel Webster asking Congress to approve sending "an Agent or Commissioner to Greece, whenever the President shall deem it expedient" (1903, 5:60). Webster's statement in support of this proposal calls forth all the emerging enthusiasm for the democracy of Athens:

> An occasion which calls attention to a spot so distinguished, so connected with interesting recollections, as Greece, may naturally create something of warmth and enthusiasm. In a grave, political discussion, however, it is necessary that those feelings should be chastised. I shall endeavor properly to repress them.

Of course, being the orator he is, he cannot. He continues:

> We must, indeed, fly beyond the civilized world; we must pass the dominion of law and the boundaries of knowledge . . . if we would separate ourselves entirely from the influence of all those memorials of herself which ancient Greece has transmitted. . . . This free form of government, this popular assembly, the common council held for the common good—where have we contemplated its earliest models? This practice of free debate and public discussion, the contest of mind with mind, and that popular eloquence, which . . . would move the stones of the Capitol,—whose was the language in which all these were first exhibited? Even the edifice in which we assemble, these proportioned columns, . . . remind us that Greece has existed, and that we, like the rest of mankind, are greatly her debtors. (1903, 5:61)

No longer is the popular regime of ancient Athens intended to frighten, to conjure up images of chaos and disorder, as in the *Federalist Papers* or in Hobbes. Rather, it has now become the marvelous model of popular government and of the reasoned exchange of ideas.

In England around the same time, in the 1820s, the Philosophical Radicals, arguing for the expansion of the franchise,
tried to use ancient democracy to move England to a more democratic regime, a move which would allow England to recapture for
itself the cultural brilliance to which Athenian democracy had
given birth. Previously, Sparta with its harsh discipline and military prowess had provided the appropriate model for Englishmen.
The histories of Greece written by English authors in the
eighteenth century emphasize the horrors of the democratic
regime of Athens while praising Sparta. In the words of Temple
Stanyan's *The Grecian History* (1751), in the Sparta given laws by Ly-
curgus, "Every Member of the State had nothing to do but to
attend the Publick. . . . They sacrific'd all sorts of Luxury to
the Liberty of the Mind. . . . Their Kings valu'd themselves
upon their Subjection to it, and distinguish'd themselves only
by a stricter Obedience" (1751, 1:94). To explain the downfall of
Sparta, Stanyan complains about the "Inspectors" who were "to
inquire into the Conduct both of the Magistracy and the People"
(1751, 1:94).

> [T]hey were chiefly to protect the Liberties of the People; who
> therefore chose them out of their own Body, without distinction of
> Birth, or Fortune, it being a sufficient Qualification, that they were
> bold, and popular. . . . However moderate their Power at first was,
> in the process of time it was so enlarg'd, that Affairs of the last
> consequence pass'd through their Hands. . . . By which means they
> seem'd to have erected a sort of Tyranny, which threaten'd greater
> Disorders than those they were design'd to remedy" (1751, 1:94).

According to Stanyan, Athens suffered from popular government even earlier. After the expulsion of the tyrant Hippias in the
sixth century, "the People wrested too great a Share of the Government into their Hands: So that things were carry'd by Tumult
and Faction; and they were seldom free from as great or worse
Disorders than those they complain'd of under their Kings" (1751,

1:202). In the Preface to his second volume Stanyan observes "how much it is to the honour of *Greece*, that so many Nations have laid claim to her as their common Mother," but according to him they have not always done well when they imitated the political structures of the ancients. "[I]n *Sparta* the Power of the Kings was too much restrain'd," but in "*Athens* the Power of the People was too excessive." Stanyan concludes that the English monarchical regime is not only better than all European regimes but also all ancient ones as well. He apologizes for the digression, "But in speaking of the *Grecian* Governments, and of those which have been grafted upon them, I could not, as an *Englishman*, resist the Temptation of saying something in Preference of our own" (1751, 2:Preface).

John Gillies, in a dedication "To the King" in his *History of Ancient Greece, Its Colonies and Conquests* (1786), says: "The History of Greece exposes the dangerous turbulence of Democracy, and arraigns the despotism of Tyrants. By describing the incurable evils inherent in every form of Republican policy, it evinces the inestimable benefits, resulting to Liberty itself, from the lawful dominion of hereditary Kings, and the steady operation of well-regulated Monarchy" (1831, iii). Commenting about Pericles' withdrawal from the assembly in his early years, Gillies notes: "But the superior talents of Pericles, which in a well regulated government, would have increased his influence, had well nigh occasioned his ruin in a turbulent and suspicious democracy" (1831, 160).

William Mitford, according to Frank Turner, was the most widely read and influential historian of ancient regimes from this period. His history told of the profound danger that the democratic regime of Athens posed for a stable, free, and legitimate regime. The 1838 edition to which I had access included "A Short Account of the Author" by his brother, in which we learn that Mitford's study of Grecian history convinced him "in believing that the forms of government adopted in the best constituted Grecian states, often the subject of youthful eulogy, were not suited to the extensive territory and the free condition of the inhabitants of the British Islands." His work thus becomes a warning about "the evils arising from all the forms of government adopted in the different states of Greece" (1838, xvii). Throughout the text, Mitford condemns Athenian democracy, calling it an "OCHLOCRACY, Mob-rule" (1838, 1:253), "that turbulent form of rule" (1838, 1:365), "A Tyranny in the Hands of the People" (1838, 4:10), and quoting Aristotle, "absolute Democracy is Tyranny" (1838, 4:33). He finds "marks of kindred between Turkish despotism and Athenian democracy" (1838, 4:20), and claims: "It was as dangerous to be rich under the Athenian democracy as under the Turkish despotism" (1838, 4:28). The freedom inherent in English institutions comes not from a classical heritage of Athenian democracy, but is "derived," according to Mitford "from German forests" and was "arranged by the great Alfred in days of the deepest barbarism" (1838, 1:364).

In 1846 John Stuart Mill, reviewing a new history of Greece written by George Grote (of whom more in a moment), reacts to Mitford's hostile treatment of Athens in this way:

> But Mitford's narrative, written and published during the wildest height of Antijacobin phrensy, is vitiated by an intensity of prejudice against whatever bears the name or semblance of popular institutions, which renders his representation of Graecian phaenomena not only false, but in many particulars the direct contrary of the truth. Athenian institutions, and the great Athenian people, to whom mankind owe a debt such as they owe to no other assemblage of men that ever existed, are studiously degraded by imputing to them not only the faults they really had, but those from which all the monuments of the time conspire to prove that they were peculiarly and preeminently exempt. (1846, 867–68)

In contrast, Mill praises the far more sympathetic work of Grote (1846, 1869), but before Grote wrote his history it was Mitford's in the 1820s and 1830s that was "in possession of the educational field, as well in the universities as in family circles" (Bain 1873, 12). And, as Turner notes, "[h]is work was immediately incorporated into tracts against the French Revolution" (1981, 204). George Grote, the author of the history Mill praised in contrast to Mitford's, was a "faithful disciple" of James Mill (Hamburger 1965, 8), a self-avowed Benthamite, and a leader of the Philosophical Radicals in the House of Commons in the 1830s. His history is a massive twelve-volume work which replaced Mitford's as the definitive history of ancient Greece. In contrast to the eighteenth-century historians' assessment of Athenian democracy as the source of turbulence and tyranny, as no different from Turkish despotism, Grote portrayed the democracy of Athens in the most glowing terms. He wrote of how "the fresh-planted democracy" brings "the growth of Athenian power, and . . . the still more miraculous development of Athenian energy" (1851, 4:237–38). His analysis of Athenian democracy identifies the "transforming cause" as "the grand and new idea of the sovereign People, composed of free and equal citizens—or liberty and equality, to use words which so profoundly moved the French nation half a century ago" (1851, 4:239). Grote becomes almost ecstatic:

> Democracy in Grecian antiquity possessed the privilege, not only of kindling an earnest and unanimous attachment to the constitution in the bosoms of the citizens, but also of creating an energy of public and private action, such as could never be obtained under an oligarchy. . . . the theory of democracy was pre-eminently seductive; creating in the mass of the citizens an intense positive attachment, and disposing them to voluntary action and suffering on its behalf, such as no coercion on the part of other governments could extort. (1851, 4:239–40)

Grote recognizes that "democracy happens to be unpalatable to most modern readers," but the reason for this is that they have turned to Aristophanic caricatures rather than Periclean speeches. To study those speeches is to find a people energetic, dedicated, courageous, and free.

In Grote's review of Mitford's history, he foreshadows his own treatment of Athenian democracy in his history:

> had it not been for democracy, and that approximation to democracy which a numerous and open aristocracy presents, this wonderful precocity of intellectual development among the Greeks would have been impracticable. . . . Publicity and constant discussion of all matters relating to the general interest—accessibility of the public esteem, which could not be thoroughly monopolized by any predominant few—intense demand for those great political qualities which are fitted to command the respect and assent of the general community—encouragement to eloquence, and to all those acquirements which eloquence presupposes, as well as to that system of instruction and mental philosophy which follows in its train—all these characteristics were to be found in the democracies more completely than in any other Grecian governments.[13]

Not only is Athenian democracy politically worthy, "it is to democracy alone (and to that sort of open aristocracy which is, practically, very similar to it), that we owe that unparalleled brilliance and diversity of individual talent."[14]

John Stuart Mill, in turn, wrote a series of reviews of Grote's own *History*. In the second such review he comments:

> The superior nobleness and superior gentleness combined, in which Athens shone preëminent among all states Greek or barbarian . . . Mr. Grote unhesitatingly ascribes to the superiority of her institutions: first, to her unlimited Democracy; and secondly, to the wise precautions, unknown to the other free states of Greece, by which the sagacity of Solon and of Cleisthenes has guarded the workings of Athenian institutions. (1847, 1084)

And Mill concludes that the great glory of Grote's *History* will be "the triumphant vindication of the Athenian Democracy" (1847,

1084). Mill notes in a review of Grote's next set of volumes that he has quoted a particular passage at length because "the view here incidentally presented of some points in the character and disposition of the Athenian Many, will afford to readers who only know Athens and Greece through the medium of writers like Mitford, some faint idea of how much they have to unlearn" (1849, 1125).

Alexander Bain, the editor of Grote's minor works, agrees that there "can be little doubt that the persistent denunciations of Grecian democracy, of which Mitford's book is a notable sample, were kept up for the sake of their application to modern instances; and Mr. Grote, by his vindication of Athens, has powerfully counterworked one of the machinations for retarding the growth of popular government in the present day" (1873, 16). So successful was Grote's refashioning of the vision of ancient democracy, Turner argues, that the Britons of the nineteenth century envisioned themselves as closer to the Athenians of the fifth century B.C. than to the British of the eighteenth century—a sentiment captured in a wonderfully foolish line from John Stuart Mill: "The battle of Marathon, even as an event in English history, is more important than the battle of Hastings. If the issue of that day had been different, the Britons and the Saxons might still have been wandering in the woods" (quoted in Momigliano 1952, 7).

Moving to the twentieth century in England, we find the English historian Alfred Zimmern preparing the second edition of *The Greek Commonwealth: Politics and Economics in Fifth Century Athens* just at the brink of the First World War. He prefaces the edition with the following reflections:

> While the book has been passing through the press war has broken out, bringing Great Britain face to face, for the first time since she has become a Democracy, with the full ultimate meaning of the civic responsibilities, both of thought and action, with which, in the narrower field of the City-State, the fifth-century Athenians

were so familiar. Greek ideas and Greek inspiration can help us today . . . in the work of deepening and extending the range and the meaning of Democracy and Citizenship, Liberty and Law. ([1911] 1922, 6)

And during the First World War, excerpts from Pericles' Funeral Oration were displayed on placards in England, arousing the modern democrats of Britain to identify with the free Athenians of the ancient democracy and thus more effectively fight the Germans. As Turner describes it: "The spirit and values of the ancient Athenian polis so memorably set forth by Pericles symbolized in the minds of many educated people the social and political solidarity to which the modern British democracy should aspire" (1981, 187).

In both America and England, then, the model of Athenian democracy was transformed in the political imagination. From a regime that turned the mob into a tyrant, causing turmoil and oppression, it became the glorious vision of nobility, freedom and equality to which politicians and journalists could turn as they argued for the support of democracy abroad (as Daniel Webster did for the Greeks rebelling from Turkish despotism) and at home (as they argued for the extension of the franchise and the elimination of intermediary filters between the people and elected officials). The stories of Athens in the political thought of England and America differ, of course, in their focus and emphasis, but in both places the transformation is radical, taking us from the forests of Germany to the agora of Athens, and the changing view accompanies the drive towards greater democratization of the respective political regimes.

V

If we move to the mid-twentieth century, democratic Athens, criticized by some for its slaves and the exclusion of women, nevertheless remains the paradigm of the good polity, despite all the social, territorial, and technological transformations of the last two and a half millennia. But Athens is now used to point out weaknesses in regimes that consider themselves democratic. Hannah Arendt is perhaps one of the most powerful examples here. She turns to Athenian democracy as the model of how democracies ought to work in contrast to what we find today. According to Arendt, ancient democracy provided the realm in which, in her words, "men could show who they really and inexchangeably were" (1958, 41). A recent study of Arendt's thought begins appropriately, I believe, with quotes from Pericles' Funeral Oration, brief reference to Athenian democracy, and then suggests: "Periclean Athens and its celebration of the public life of the *polis*—its democratic temper, the virile virtuosity of its citizens, its keen passion for competitive excellence—is the powerful image at the heart of Hannah Arendt's political theory" (Dossa 1989, vii).[15]

The glory of the ancient world of the Greek city for Arendt was that its equality was not based on conformity. She calls the Greek city-state "the most individualist and least conformable body politic known to us" (1958, 43). It is important to remember, in this age when we may find some questioning excessive individualism at the expense of community, that Arendt's language is the language of praise, not castigation (cf. 1958, 194). According to Arendt, politics in the Athenian polis was "agonal," conflictual, where individuals sought distinction and thus, in her view, the "public realm . . . was reserved for individuality" (1958, 41). To support her reading of the ancient city, Arendt turns to Homer, to a phrase often repeated in his epics, "always to be the best and to rise above others"; that several hundred years passed between the composition of the Homeric epics and the rise of the democratic polis is explained away by the note that "Homer was 'the educator of Hellas'" (1958, 41n. 34).

In her model that makes a deep distinction between behavior and action, the modern world where humans labor in the economic and social sphere "only for the sake of life and nothing else" has lost the capacity of ancient activity, the authentic concern with immortality. "The *polis* was supposed to multiply the occasions to win 'immortal fame,' . . . to multiply the chances for everybody to distinguish himself, to show in deed and word who he was in his unique distinctness" ([1954] 1977, 197). To show distinction one needed the equality and the freedom of the ancient polis, but these terms as Arendt uses them do not meld easily with modern usage. Returning to the Greek concept of equality before the law, *isonomy* (which she distinguishes from democratic rule), she chooses a constructed equality of property owners rather than an equality of all men grounded in nature. "Equality existed only in this specifically political realm, where men met one another as citizens and not as private persons. . . . The equality of the Greek polis, its isonomy, was an attribute of the polis and not of men" (1963, 23).

Describing the Athenian polis in her essay "Tradition and the Modern Age," Arendt explicitly excludes the majority of more recent versions of ancient democracy and emphasizes instead that citizens "were citizens only insofar as they possessed leisure time . . . those who labored were not citizens" ([1954] 1977, 19). Athens for Arendt is not the vision with which to move the modern world to greater egalitarianism, as it has been understood in the post-Lockean or post-Declaration of Independence mode of natural equality. Rather, the ancient city demonstrates the virtue of a created egalitarianism in the service of freedom, a condition possible only among constructed, not natural, equals: "The life of a free man needed the presence of others. Freedom itself needed therefore a place where people could come together—the agora, the market place, or the polis" (1963, 24). The one who rules over others (the tyrant or the despot) was not free since "he had deprived himself of those peers in whose company he could have been free" (1963, 24). It is not ancient democracy that Arendt holds up for the modern world; that democracy, simply, was "majority rule . . . [a term] originally coined by those who were opposed to isonomy and who meant to say: . . . it is the worst form of government, rule by the demos" (1963, 23). Rather, she presents us with a political model of created equals in interaction through speech—not violence—with one another.

In her return to the ancient polity, then, Arendt differs in her motivation from those writers discussed above: she finds there not a political system that draws its authority from "the sovereign people," or one where the middle class and the poor were drawn into political life. Rather, the envisioned polis provided the arena for action among equals in a realm of freedom, action that transformed man from a laboring animal to a human being who can give expression to his individuality. Athenian democracy is used by Arendt to inveigh against a world that ignores "action" in favor of "labor" and has transformed the public arena of distinguished men into the "'administration of things' . . . of interest only to a cook, or at best to those 'mediocre minds' whom Nietzsche thought best qualified for taking care of public affairs" ([1954] 1977, 19). In Arendt's version—or should we say "vision"?—of the polis, the citizen did not prefer his farm to extended stays in the city of freedom, nor were citizens participating in the public sphere aiming at venal profit rather than immortality through speech. There were only those who sought eternal fame grounded in the open forum of the assembly and the agora.

M. I. Finley's compact and wonderfully readable *Democracy: Ancient and Modern* published in 1973 and reprinted in 1985 has perhaps done the most to articulate for the present generation "the model of ancient democracy" as distinct from modern democracy. To present the popular view of modern democracy, Finley turned to the social scientists of the 1960s, those whom we may call the "theorists of apathy," who applauded apathy in the modern state for the stability it provided. The 1950s and early 1960s had left a world recoiling from the horrors of fascism. Reactions were so strong that a lead article in *Political Studies*, the most prestigious English political science journal, entitled "In Defense of Apathy," argued that "many of the ideas connected with the general theme of a Duty to Vote belong properly to the totalitarian camp and are out of place in the vocabulary of liberal democracy."[16] This was Morris Jones defending what many others—Schumpeter already in 1942, Lipset, the Dahl of the 1960s (though not of the 1990s), Bernard Berelson— had defended as the benefits of apathy. Against these modern "democratic" theorists, Finley brings the model of participatory Athens where "politics, the art of reaching decisions by public discussion and then obeying those decisions" was discovered (1973, 13–14). He writes of Athens as the "case-study of how political leadership and popular participation succeeded in co-existing . . . without . . . the apathy and ignorance exposed by public opinion experts" (1973, 33). Finley avoids any absurd claims that we should try to recapture ancient democracy but asks that we consider whether "new forms of popular partici-pation, in the Athenian spirit though not in the Athenian sub-stance . . . need to be invented" (1973, 36).

In a later essay on "Politics and Political Theory," Finley notes that the Greeks took a radical step, a double one: "they lo-cated the source of authority in the *polis*, in the community itself, and they decided on policy in open discussion, eventually by voting, by counting heads." And, he writes (and I read ap-proval in his language), "That is politics, and fifth-century Greek drama and historiography reveal how far politics had come to dominate Greek culture" (1981, 22). While the behavioral revolu-tion in political science may have its faults, it has taught us the difference between prescription and what happens. Anyone who lives in a democratic society knows that life is not that simple. Heads are not simply counted; power, wealth, and interest do not yield easily to open, reasoned discussion—neither now nor then. That a scholar of Finley's distinction should remain content with such a description of the polis suggests perhaps the almost magical attraction of the supposed wonder of ancient democracy.

Cynthia Farrar, in a more recent work entitled *The Origins of Democratic Thinking*, is not quite so restrained as Finley and shows how powerful the hold of the vision of democratic Athens is even in the modern age. She writes:

> It is democracy, as conceived and lived by Athenians in the fifth century B.C., that offers at least the possibility of healing this spiritual and social fragmentation. . . . All citizens were thought to be capable of appreciating and feeling the connection between their interests and those of the community because they were constantly, as active political participants, asked to assess and interpret that connection. . . . The challenge is to turn toward the example of a living democracy, ancient Athens. (1988, 274–76)

In the mid- and late-twentieth century, the legacy of ancient democracy resounds with calls to recover a politics we often fear has been lost, despite the fact that we are still plagued in our study of that democracy by the uncertainty of the historical record and the lack of any author from ancient Athens whom we may describe as a democratic theorist.

It was in France of the nineteenth century that one already began to hear rumblings about the apotheosis of ancient democracy. Benjamin Constant, for instance, in his celebrated lecture on ancient and modern liberty of 1819, portrayed Athens as a large trading state offering greater individual liberty than Sparta or Rome, but still "the individual was much more subservient to the supremacy of the social body of Athens, than he is in any of the free states of Europe today" ([1819] 1988, 316). Later in the century Fustel de Coulanges in *The Ancient City* used a detailed and extended (though now highly suspect) study of ancient social and political relations to express similar concerns about the loss of individuality. He warns in 1864: "The last eighty years have clearly shown that one of the great difficulties which impede the march of modern society is the habit which it has of always keeping Greek and Roman antiquity before its eyes" ([1864] 1980, 3). For Fustel the ancient city, democratic or oligarchic, was limited by the noose of religion which stifled any individual freedom; it was a world that did not provide for any individual immortality such as Arendt envisioned but rather offered only complete oppression. But Fustel's own agenda of demonstrating the positive role of Christianity in guaranteeing a free society, his dependence on ideas as the causative agents in world history, and his questionable scholarship mitigated the power of his critique.

Instead, we are left today for the most part (slavery and the status of women emphatically aside) with an amorphous vision of the perfection of ancient democracy where "freedom" allowed the arts to flourish, where men eagerly participated in a public world seeking immortality through public speech, where the will of the sovereign people was put into practice, where care for the community did not work in opposition to individual interest, where, in Finley's terms, they decided policy in open discussion by counting heads (or hands), and as we heard but a few years ago from I. F. Stone (1988), Socrates' execution happened only because of Socrates' foolish antidemocratic fervor, not because of any faults in the democracy itself. Ancient democracy may thus serve as a model for heuristic or more often rhetorical purposes, but the failure to take seriously the complexity of ancient democracy and the historical evidence about how it functioned means, I believe, that its theoretical significance may be lost. As an amorphous concept inadequately situated in the world of ancient Athens, it can lead to amorphous theories and provide meaningless prescriptions based on visions that may be no more than romantic longings—whether for or against Athenian democracy as a model for our own lives.

The difficulty that the mythmakers create for us is that they do not let us see clearly the issues and questions about democracy as raised by the historians and philosophers of Athens. In the following chapters I hope to illuminate how the ancients help us understand democracy, not in the false language of a sovereign people expressing freely its will, but in terms that derive directly from their own experience of the Athenian political regime in action.[17] Part of the challenge for me will be to shake off the encrustations of scholarship that have relied on the romanticized visions of Athenian democracy of the last century in order to probe the core of the ancients' interpretations of democracy. I do not wish to present the authors I discuss as advocates or opponents of democracy. Herodotus is not simply a fan of democracy and the free Greeks; Thucydides is not simply a severe critic; Plato is not simply a defender of hierarchy or, more crassly, aristocracy; and Aristotle is not simply the spokesman of a participatory citizenship, as Arendt would have it. Careful readings of the works of these authors reveal the complexity of their responses to the Athenian regime and the complex lessons they teach about democracy. They let us understand the underlying principles and assumptions that we must confront as we defend and try to implement democratic principles in the modern world.

CHAPTER 2

Herodotus, Democracy, and Equality

I

The potential for participation in the decision-making processes of a political regime defines for many the essence of democratic institutions. Contemporary debates in political science explore how it is we are to define that participation: is a vote every four years adequate to say that we participate or do we need to read the *New York Times* and the *Washington Post* daily and write letters to members of Congress to say that we participate? Political theorists also explore what we might consider meaningful participation and the degree to which participation is an expression of autonomy and engagement or simply subjection to community norms. Thus, it is not surprising that when contemporary historians study the world of Athenian democracy, they study it from the perspective of participation, using the new techniques of the social scientist as well as the older efforts of textual analysis to understand how participation expressed itself in the first democratic regime.

As I turn to the ancients themselves in this chapter, I will suggest that their questions are quite different from our own, that they do not focus on the theoretical significance of participation.

They have other questions that control their response to the democratic model and help us think about the challenges and the possibilities of democratic regimes. Herodotus only uses the word *dēmokratia* (or variants) three times in his lengthy *Histories*. Yet we find in his writings a fascination with the question of equality—whether it is natural or constructed, whether regimes can be built on principles of equality or whether they must have unequal distributions of power. He himself provides no final statement; he is an observer who delights in viewing the many different human types and organizations he encounters during his travels. Nevertheless, beneath that delight is a commitment to an equality of human beings, all of whom are worthy of comment and our inquiries. Herodotus is not a democratic theorist as such, but his interest in equality, which lies at the core of democratic institutions, makes him at the very least of interest to those of us who study ancient democracy.[1]

Our problem in the study of Athenian democracy begins on a linguistic level. We today look to the institutions of Athens and say that the Athenians lived in a democracy, but it was not until quite late in the history of those institutions, in what we blithely call Athenian democracy, that the word *dēmokratia* surfaces as a regular inhabitant of Attic literature. Stockton comments: "[T]he first occurrence of the word in surviving Greek literature is in Herodotus' *History* (6.43, 131), which he was writing during the third quarter of the fifth century" (1990, 1). Sealey concludes his extensive study of the word by noting that *dēmokratia* has only minimal value as a descriptive empirical term since assemblies were hardly the exclusive practice of democratic regimes (1974). Ober dates the use of *dēmokratia* as "the standard term to describe the Athenian form of government" to the 440s B.C., close to seventy years after the reforms of Cleisthenes supposedly introduced democracy to the Athenians (1989a, 82).[2]

So far as we can tell, it seems that the term *isonomia* rather than *dēmokratia* described for the Athenians the regime instituted by

Cleisthenes.[3] As Sealey phrases it, *isonomia* is the euphemism, *dēmokratia* the blunt term (1974, 274). The euphemism draws on the foundations in the equality of sharing rule, the "blunt term" refers to the consequences. As Vlastos writes (1953, 352): "[W]hat the word [*isonomia*] asserts is not merely that the laws should be equally upheld, but that they should be equal in the wholly different sense of defining the equal share of all the citizens in the control of the state." Vlastos gives a somewhat different twist to Sealey's distinction between the "blunt" *dēmokratia* and the euphemism *isonomia* when he eloquently comments: "For while *Demokratia* does no more than describe a fact, *Isonomia* expresses an idea, indeed a whole set of ideas, by which partisans of democracy *justified* the rule of the people" (1953, 347, emphasis in the original). Democracy as participation is based on the normative principle of equality, that not one, but all, share in the structure of the community in which they live.[4]

Within the Athenian *ecclēsia*, or assembly, the principle of *isēgoria* or equal opportunity to speak maintained the equality at the base of Athens' political regime. Though the *ecclēsia* is at the center of the Athenian regime, the problem of ancient democracy had little to do with the translation of the "will" of a sovereign people into the policy of the city, as we of the modern world have come to conceptualize democracy. Despite personifications of *hoi polloi* and the *dēmos*, despite the phrase *edokei dēmoi* ("it seems best to the *dēmos*") to express the decrees approved in the assembly, it is no more likely that the sovereign people of Athens had a single will than that such a thing exists today. The problem was not even aggregation of disparate wills, but rather how to define who was equal and thus included in the community that shared in the decisions about shared concerns; who enjoyed equally a shared opportunity to speak, and, in contrast, who was considered unequal, whether superior and thus above the law or inferior and thus not to be engaged in making laws which were to govern others. The Greek authors were always working from what

I shall call a "constructed equality" rather than the natural equality that we, raised in the language of the Declaration of Independence, consider to be a "self-evident truth." It was the assertion of equality among some that lay at the foundation of ancient democracy, not the assumption of equality among all. The challenge for those looking at democratic institutions was to identify the boundaries of citizenship and explore their validity.[5]

Herodotus, writing in a period when the issues concerning equality, inclusion, and exclusion were coalescing, helps us recognize the complexity and difficulties of equality as a universal or as a localized principle, as natural or as constructed, as a principle that could be institutionalized or that resisted institutionalization. In Book 5 of the *Histories* he reports the comments of a certain Corinthian, Socles by name, who suggests that to abolish *isokratia* (equality of power) in cities in favor of instituting a tyranny would be the equivalent of turning the world upside down, with the sky below and the earth above (5.92). Socles sees men sharing power equally as a natural phenomenon. To deny equality is to deny that the sun rises. Nevertheless, despite this assertion by one of Herodotus' characters, the many stories told of tyrants in the *Histories* indicate that even if equality of power in cities were according to nature, there is no guarantee that nature will prevail to ensure that this equality will be preserved. Indeed, mostly it is not preserved, and Herodotus throughout his work explores the relationship of nature, equality, and convention. He never demonstrates the truth of Socles' assertion that *isokratia* is by nature; rather, he affirms its normative value, while recognizing its limits and all that militates against its institutionalization.

Democracy (which Herodotus barely discusses) becomes one way of attempting to institutionalize this favored equality, but in so doing it also raises its own difficulties, in terms of definition (which will also plague Plato and Aristotle) and in terms of the distribution of authority. Even after those who are to be equal within any community are identified, the city, be it Athens or any political community, introduces inequalities of authority that undermine the fragile equality at the heart of the democratic institutions of the city. This is the difficulty that we find reflected continuously in the ancient theorists' consideration of democracy. It is not the issue of participation that has weighed so heavily on our own image of the ancients and of those who have praised or criticized the Athenians over the centuries, but rather how equals are to rule themselves. And it is here that Herodotus often makes us aware of just how intractable this problem is—at the same time that he sees equality as the basis for the noblest of regimes.

In Book 3 Herodotus tells the story of one Maeandrius, the successor to the tyrant Polycrates of Samos. Maeandrius wanted to be the "justest" (*dikaiotatos*) of men. He told an assembly of all the citizens that the despotism of Polycrates had never pleased him and that he planned to place rule "in the middle" (*es meson*) and "to introduce *isonomia*" among them. But there arose among the people one who accused Maeandrius of being base, and this man urged the assembly of men to refuse to give him the modest sum of money he had requested from Polycrates' estate. At this, Maeandrius realized that someone else would become tyrant in place of him, and so he decided to remain the ruler of Samos (3.142–43). Justice, according to Maeandrius, is the equality of rule among his fellow citizens, what Socles had claimed was according to nature. But Maeandrius discovers that this justice is not an easy virtue to exercise, that equality, however "natural" it may be, must fight against the equally natural desire for precedence.

Often Herodotus' work is read as the opposition between the free Greeks and the tyranny of the East, with victory crowning the free (and democratic) Greeks. I find, however, in Herodotus what Richard Mulgan finds in Greek thought in general: "If there is an organizing concept in Greek democratic thought it is not freedom so much as equality (*isotēs*), with its specific cognates *isonomia* . . . and *isēgoria*, equal speaking rights. This may indicate that equality rather than freedom carried most weight as a political principle" (1984, 12–13). As noted above, seldom does the word *dēmokratia* appear in the *Histories*, and Herodotus does not write primarily as an Athenian or primarily about Athenian democracy.[6] The complications posed by an equality, whether natural or constructed, institutionalized or submerged, run through his varied and wide-ranging text, and this is what I shall address below.

II

By referring to Herodotus in this chapter, and Thucydides in the next, as "historians," I yield to a long tradition that has given them this title, with all the nineteenth-century intellectual baggage that that title brings.[7] Yes, both Herodotus and Thucydides tell us about events that occurred in the past, about individuals who lived in the past, and about cities and nations that existed long ago, but my concern here is to treat them as theorists rather than as historians. The word "theorist" comes from the Greek *theoria*, a looking at. When the Solon of Herodotus' work sails away from Athens after having given to his city a new set of laws, he sets out for the sake of *theoria* (1.29), perhaps to be translated "sight-seeing," as David Grene does in his translation (Herodotus 1987), but more generally just as observing or seeing the world beyond the confines of Athens. As with Solon, so too with Herodotus. He engages in *theoria*, a looking at, an observing of a multitude of peoples and of customs. But both he and Thucydides do much more than look. They analyze and explore implications; they (Herodotus openly, Thucydides less openly) evaluate and pass judgment; they interpret. The process of *theoria*, observation, is in no way passive, to be contrasted, as in modern thought, with *praxis* or activity, and with Herodotus it is precisely its active role that engages us. He questions and we question. He makes us see more than the events or the countries or the kings and their advisers in his stories; he makes us see our own politics, democratic or otherwise, by forcing us to ask his questions and not our own, thus making us aware of what is universal out of the many particulars that he observes and reflects upon.

Herodotus' understanding of political regimes, of the implications of social organization, more often emerges from the short stories he tells, the anecdotes, the customs he describes, the personalities to whom he introduces us, than from that great confrontation between East and West that takes up the second half of the book. There are, of course, the grand battles, Thermopylae, Marathon, Salamis, that have fired the imagination, but then there is also the brief tale (like the story of Maeandrius cited above), told quickly with a modicum of commentary, if any at all, that helps to give meaning to the grander struggles. Herodotus writes not only of the greatness of one regime, but also of the various forms of greatness possible for other political regimes. It is by looking at his brief stories and recognizing his openness to various forms of virtue that we can best learn from him about our topic.

As noted above, many too easily think of Herodotus' *Histories* as recounting the great clash between the enslaved East and the free Greeks led by democratic Athens. For instance, the blurb for the commonly used Penguin translation notes that Herodotus' "main theme" is the struggle of Greece against Persia "with its underlying conflict between the absolutism of the East and the free institutions of the West" (Herodotus [1954] 1972). Or the Modern Library edition introduced by R. B. Godolphin notes that Cleisthenes' liberal policies were "essential to the development of Athenian democracy. It was the rapid development of the new constitution which enabled Athens to play such a large part in the struggle to repulse the Persian[s] and maintain free institutions" (Herodotus 1942, xviii). Donald Kagan in his study of

Greek political thought likewise writes: "Herodotus was power-fully impressed by the Greeks' successful defense of their free-dom against Persian attack, which was the theme of his great work" (1965, 65). Kagan adds a bit later: "The democratic Athens of Cleisthenes is singled out as a paradigm of the wondrous con-sequences of freedom" (1965, 68). How and Wells, almost a cen-tury ago, in their extensive textual commentary on Herodotus, remark: "H. here, as usual, champions freedom and constitu-tional government against tyranny" ([1912] 1989, 5:78).[8] The source of their reading of Herodotus' work rests on a powerful passage from the fifth book:

> It is clear that not only in one thing but in every way is *isēgoria* [equality in public speech] a worthy thing [Note: Herodotus does not use *dēmokratia*]; the Athenians, while they were under the rule of the tyranny, were in no way any better than those who lived around her in the affairs of war; after they cast off the tyranny, they were by far the foremost. It is clear that when they were held down they were unwilling, as working for a master, but when they were freed (*eleutheronthenton*) each one was eager to work for himself. (5.78)

George Grote, in a fashion similar to How and Wells, quotes in full the same passage (claiming it is "too emphatic to be omit-ted") immediately after commenting on the "fruit of the fresh-planted democracy," i.e., "the growth of Athenian power and the still more miraculous development of Athenian energy." He concludes, after the Herodotean passage: "Stronger expressions cannot be found to depict the rapid improvement wrought in the Athenian people by their new democracy" (1851, 4:176–77).

Though this passage from the fifth book is often used to illus-trate the equation between freedom and democracy in Athens in Herodotus' thought, such a claim is too simple, even leaving aside that *dēmokratia* does not appear.[9] Even Kagan feels he must qualify himself and adds to his just-cited praise of Athens: "Does this mean that freedom exists only in democratic states? Surely not, for the Spartans, living under the closest state supervision, are also free (*History* vii, 104), and so too are all the Greek cities arrayed against Persia, whatever their form of government" (1965, 68).

For Herodotus, it is not only the Greek cities arrayed against the Persians who are free. It is the Medes fighting against the Assyrians at the beginning of Book 1; they, "casting off their slavery (*ten doulosunen*) became free (*eleutherouthesan*)" (1.95). It is the Persians themselves, under the leadership of Cyrus, who long for and eventually get freedom from the Medes. It is the Egyptians who are freed when the priest Hephaestus is overthrown (2.147). Sparta with its kings is free; the nomadic Scythians are free. The Athenians too are free. It is not, however, their democratic institutions (which Herodotus does not discuss), but the expulsion of Hippias and the assassination of Hipparchus that make them free. The Spartans who do not enjoy a democracy are free, but they do fear that should the Athenians likewise become free (*eleutheroi*), they would become equal in strength to the Spartans, whereas held down by a tyranny they would be "weak and ready to be ruled" (5.91). The freedom from tyranny which the Spartans enjoy is the key to strength here, not the institution of a democratic regime. Democracy as it appears in Herodotus' work is not the analogue of freedom. Freedom is a much wider concept: it means not being ruled by an individual who is (or sees himself as) superior, or by a nation that is stronger.

To read the *Histories* as simply a grand battle between Persian despotism and the freedom of Greek democracy unfortunately ignores the complexities of Herodotus' stories. Let us begin our study of "democracy" in Herodotus not by looking at the free Athenians only but by focusing on a number of the stories that have nothing to do with Athens, its democratic political institutions, or the identity between freedom and democracy, but that address the issue of the equality that lies at the heart of democracy and its concerns.

III

First, Cyrus, the liberator of the Persians from the rule of the Medes, embarks on a program of domination and conquers the city of Babylonia. In Herodotus' *Histories,* no tale of conquest is told without extensive reporting on the people and the customs of the conquered city. And so we hear about Babylonian customs, those that are admirable and those that are not. The following is the custom that in Herodotus' opinion is the "very wisest" (*sophotatos*) and "most beautiful" (*kallistos*) (1.196): In every village, the girls who are of an age to be married are brought together and the men who wish to be married bid on the girls. It is like an auction for wives, but before we let our feminist hackles rise and before we start judging Herodotus as a proponent of slavery let us consider how this "very wisest" of customs is organized. The auctioneer begins with the most beautiful girl, who brings in a great deal of money. He then auctions the next most beautiful girl and so on down the line of beautiful girls. It is the rich men who are able to bid and they use their money to buy themselves beautiful wives. But there are also poor men in the city as well as girls who are not so beautiful. The Babylonians arranged that the poor men were paid to marry the ugly girls. Using the money received from the auction of the beautiful girls, the auctioneer would do the reverse and find men willing to be paid the least to marry the ugly girls.

Why does Herodotus consider this to be the "wisest" and "most beautiful" of customs? It equalizes. It takes differences between individuals and makes those differences irrelevant. The object is marriage for both those who are beautiful and those who are ugly, those who are rich and those who are poor. Without this custom only the beautiful and the rich would marry; the poor could not afford to marry and the ugly would not be sought after. The custom takes the advantages enjoyed by some and uses those advantages to benefit the whole community. The word "democracy," to be sure, never surfaces in the discussion of Babylonia, but the egalitarianism at the heart of the principles of ancient democracy, an egalitarianism here based not on nature but constructed by human ingenuity, is at work. Nature has not made us equal in beauty and we are not equal in wealth, but the Babylonians contrived a system that equalizes what was not equal, that allows all to achieve the same goal despite the niggardliness of a nature that creates differences among humans. Herodotus' praise of institutions that create equality emerges powerfully in this praise of the Babylonian custom. The goal of equality *against* nature is the fairest of customs among those of the East. Socles asserts an equality of sharing in power by nature within the city. The Babylonians show that a *natural* equality does not matter; we can create it in opposition to nature and make the ugliest inequality into a beautiful equality. Vlastos' discussion of the meaning of *isonomia* within the context of Athenian democracy builds on the same principle. Equality of democracy comes not from an identity based on nature or the possession of wealth, but from a capacity to share, irrespective of the qualities with which we begin. This is not to say that all are included, but a subset of citizens is made, not born, equal. And it is the laws that accomplish this equalizing.

In the description of the next custom of the Babylonians, Herodotus gives us more of a feeling of their egalitarianism. This custom he defines as the second most wise. They have no doctors. Instead, the sick are brought to the agora and everyone gives them advice about how to get well. In particular, all who have had the same illness must give advice on what led to their recovery. They approach the ill person, comfort him, and tell him what they know from personal experience, or from observing another, about how to get well. "It is not permitted to them to walk by a suffering person in silence" (1.197). This is a community without specialists. No unique knowledge inheres in any member of the community that peculiarly grants him or her the ability to heal another.[10] As in the principle behind the system of the lot for political office, as in the principle behind the participation of all citizens in the decision-making processes of the city, as in the argument of Protagoras about the distribution of political skills, no one individual stands above the others in his or her wisdom about medical affairs, or, if they do, he or she is not so superior that the community would benefit more from one individual's knowledge than the collective wisdom of all. With this custom the Babylonians acknowledge an equality grounded in nature. The challenge for the regime here is to create institutions that draw on whatever equality may really exist rather than to undermine it. But, we may note, this is only the second wisest custom since, by finding equality in nature, the custom is not opposed to nature and requires only the skill of preserving, not of creating. The regime of the Babylonians, then, made equal what was not equal by nature and reenforced what natural equality there may have been. These are the wise customs of the people conquered by and made subject to the tyrant Cyrus.

There is no claim by the Babylonians (or Herodotus) that all (wo)men are created equal (in beauty), only that custom (*nomos*) has the capacity to equalize. While nature may be unfair in her distribution of the virtue (if we may call it that) of beauty, human choice through *nomos* can counter that inequality, and in its wisdom it will do so. According to a song of Harmodius which is quoted by Vlastos (1953, 340), the tyrannicides in Athens, by ousting from power Hippias and Hipparchus, made the Athenians *isonomous*, accomplishing much the same thing as the Babylonians; whether the citizens are equal by nature or not, *isonomia* can construct equals. With the tyrants no longer in power, the Athenian regime treats as equal those who may not be so. Making no claims about natural equality, the principle of *isonomia* can posit an equality which allows each man, as Herodotus phrases it, to work for himself and not as a slave to another.

In a well-known phrase, Herodotus says that *nomos* is king

(3.38), but he also makes us aware of how tenuous is the human capacity to fight against nature, and of how the king (or *nomos*) does not always remain secure in his (its) rule. The most beautiful of the Babylonian customs, at least according to Herodotus, that which equalized natural difference, is the one which the Babylonians themselves have allowed to fall into disuse; prostitution by the daughters of the poor has come to replace the finest of customs in Babylonia. To fight natural inequality is difficult. The opposition between *nomos* and nature is strong and *nomos* does not always remain the easy victor. The beauty of the first custom and of the Athenian regime is the commitment to the construction of a beautiful equality, but it will always be a struggle against a natural inequality which king *nomos* may not always win.

The most shameful (*aischristos*, 1.199) of the Babylonian customs, according to Herodotus, in contrast perpetuates natural inequalities. It is the following: Each female in Babylonia must go to the temple of the goddess Aphrodite and wait to be chosen by a man who throws money into her lap. She must then follow him out of the temple and have intercourse with the man who has contributed money to the temple. "Once she has lain [with the man] she has paid off her debt to the goddess and she is set free to return home. The tall and the beautiful are quickly released, but those among them who are without pleasing shape remain there a long time unable to break the *nomos*. Some remain three or four years" (1.199). There is no attempt by the law to erase natural inequalities in beauty. Instead, custom works to perpetuate those inequalities and is thus judged the ugliest of customs.

Herodotus' assessment of this custom as the "ugliest" or "most shameful" makes clear his own commitment to equality, whether natural or the result of human ingenuity.[11] It is this that makes Herodotus a foe of the tyrannies of the East and an admirer of the cities of Greece. We see this vividly in his portrayal of the Greek resistance to the Persian custom of *proskunēsis*, prostration or bowing down before a Persian king.[12] He writes of two courageous Spartan youths who have agreed to go to Persia to pay the penalty for the Spartan murder of two Persian envoys. Upon arriving before the Persian king, "when the sword bearers [of the King] ordered them and asserted that it was necessary to prostrate themselves [*proskuneein*] before the King, they said that they would not do it because they were not accustomed to throw themselves headlong before any one. For it was not in their *nomoi* to prostrate themselves [*proskuneein*] before a man" (7.136). Xerxes, the Persian king in this case, tries unsuccessfully to out-argue them, claiming that as the Lacedaemonians cling to what is customary for them as a particular people who assert human equality, they do not attend to what is practiced universally among all men—a patently false claim, considering the Spartan youths who literally stand before him.

Herodotus' history is filled with this fundamental assertion of human equality where men should not have to prostrate themselves before other men, though political institutions may not always reflect and incorporate this equality. It is an equality he recognizes despite the vast differences among the people and the races and the customs that he consistently delights in reporting. His fascination with varieties of cultures and even with the appearances of the distant tribes and nations, that are so tall or so black, derives from his commitment to the fundamental unity and equality of the human species despite the differences of custom and race. It is a commitment that can be captured in regimes, democratic or otherwise, that do not enslave, that allow the human being the dignity of self-rule whether through common institutions or not. But the commitment to equality leaves open the question of authority and rule. The tyrant rules, but what happens among equals?

IV

The wife of the Spartan king Aristodemos gave birth to twins. The Spartans were eager to identify who between the two children should be king. Since the twins were the "same and equal [*homoiōn kai isōn eontōn*]," the Spartans asked the mother which one was older. She claimed not to know, but as the Spartans watched her they saw that she regularly fed and bathed one child first. That child they made their king (6.52). The Spartans could not accept the two babies as equals. One needed to be identified as different and thereby given rule even though the twins appeared to be the "same and equal."

A commitment to equality, as authors from Thomas Hobbes to Walter Lippmann have pointed out, raises the problem of leadership, and it is that issue that confronts regimes of equals, ancient or modern, and poses the real challenges to human equality. Let me discuss how two other stories in the *Histories* address this problem in a peculiarly Herodotean way. The first story tells of the rise of one-man rule among the Medes after they have become "free" from the domination of the Assyrians. It is a story of a wise or crafty or skillful (*sophos*) man named Deioces who happened to become enamored of tyrannical rule (*erastheis turannidos*, 1.96), i.e., he wished to be unequal, to be above the others. He had an ingenious way of satisfying this longing: he saw chaos and injustice around him and he decided to become known throughout the Median villages as the most straight and just judge. All came to him for just decisions in their disputes—until one day he chose not to sit in judgment anymore. It was not profitable for him to judge his neighbors' cases while neglecting his own affairs (1.97). So pillage and anomie were even greater than before until finally the Medes consulted among themselves and concluded that they could not continue living as they were and decided to establish a kingship. "And thus the countryside will be well governed and we will turn to our own affairs and will not be divided by anomie" (1.97). Thus, Deioces became king.

Thomas Hobbes and John Locke, likewise eager to turn men from public conflict to private pleasures, could hardly have told a better story, but what happens next is important for understanding the problems that face democratic egalitarians, for Deioces sets down certain conditions before he is willing to become king, i.e., to go from being an equal to a ruler. A great fortress of seven concentric walls was to be built, and inside the innermost wall was to be the castle and the treasury. Deioces was, according to Herodotus, the first to establish the custom that no one would ever be in the presence of a king and that all business would be transacted by messengers so that no one would see the king. Herodotus explains all:

> He arranged these things about himself on account of the following: so that those of the same age who were nurtured with him and who were of households not more worthless than his and who were not left behind in manly goodness, so that they, seeing him, might not become grieved and plot, and that for those who did not see him he might seem to be different [*heteros*]. (1.99)

In other words, were they to observe him, those who were his equals in family, in age, and in virtue, they would recognize that only pomp, circumstance, and seven concentric walls made him and not them the king. The differences that he had exhibited as judge were not sufficient to ensure lasting authority. The stability of the monarchical regime that had been established depended on the *appearance* of inequality, an appearance that could only be maintained if Deioces were not actually seen by those who would see themselves in the king and would thus question why an equal ruled over them. The wisdom of Deioces was nowhere more evident than in his awareness of how powerful are the claims of an equality in rule.

Herodotus' commentary on Babylonian customs indicates the value he places on equality, on using custom to create equalities where they may not exist by nature, but he points out the need of politics to create artificial inequalities as well, something that is only accomplished in Deioces' case by making the leader virtually invisible so that his equality with others escapes the notice of his subjects. Among equals, Herodotus, here at least, perceives the possibility of continuing chaos. However much equality is a goal, however much he may find in it the key to theorizing about humanity, he, like Hobbes and Locke, recognizes that equality may work against political order. The solution in the story of Deioces is not a democratic share in the rule, but a withdrawal from rule and the establishment of an artificial rule by carefully preserved inequality.

The story of Amasis, a king of Egypt, reminds us as well of how fragile is the inequality of leadership. Amasis becomes king of Egypt, but not in the most elegant of ways. When the Egyptians revolted against their king Apries, the king sent Amasis as a messenger to the rebels in order to bring them back into submission to the king. But the rebels decided that they liked Amasis better than their king and they granted him sovereignty over them. In response to the king's next messenger, sent to find out what was going on among the rebels, Amasis behaved "in an unseemly fashion" (or in Grene's more graphic translation "farted" [2.162]). When the king's messenger returned without Amasis, the king ordered (without waiting for an explanation) the messenger's ears and nose cut off. This outrageous behavior towards his own messenger, a distinguished and well-liked Egyptian, aroused the rest of the Egyptians to rebel and make Amasis their king, even though Amasis did not come from a noble background. "At first the Egyptians scorned Amasis and thought him worth very little since originally he was of the people [dēmotēs] and of a not distinguished household" (2.172). To address this problem, Amasis took a golden foot-basin, in which Amasis himself and his guests had often washed their feet, and he made from it a beautiful image of a god, about which the Egyptians made a great fuss. Calling together the Egyptians, Amasis pointed out to them that the statue which they now revered had once served as a receptacle for their vomit and their urine. "He said that he himself was similar to the foot-basin. If once he was *dēmotēs*, now he was their king and he bid them honor and respect him." As Herodotus concludes: "In this fashion he convinced the Egyptians that their slavery was just [*hōste dikaion douleuein*]" (2.172). From an original equality an inequality is created. The washbasin is restructured, just as a man of the people is made a king. There is a fluidity in nature; the exercise of the creative talent of political founders stabilizes this fluidity in a hierarchical mode. It is inequality that is constructed here.

The stories of both Amasis and Deioces suggest that there is nothing *by nature* that gives one man rule over another, that (in modern liberal terms) no one is so different from another to justify his or her rule over another. A man of the people can become king. All that change are some external attributes—perhaps a castle with seven concentric walls and a willingness to accord him (or sometimes "her" in Herodotus' *Histories*) the accouterments of authority. Along with the Babylonians who refuse to have doctors, we again see here the assertion of human equality, the denial of a natural hierarchy of rule and a sense that rule, while necessary, does not give to whoever rules any natural superiority over another. If Amasis' foot-basin could become an object of adoration once it was transformed into a statue of a god, why should we revere the authority of anyone who is nothing more than the equal to ourselves though clothed or housed in a somewhat grander style?

Recording another tale that he brings from Egypt, Herodotus tells of the period when the Egyptians had been freed from the priest Hephaestus. They could not live without a king; so they set up twelve kings and twelve provinces. These twelve kings agreed that no one would seek more than another, although there had been a prophecy that should one of them pour a libation from a bronze vessel he would become king of all Egypt. As it turns out in cases of this sort in Herodotus' *Histories*, one of the kings performs this action inadvertently. The others chase him away, but he returns and becomes the one king (2.147–55). Here, human efforts to preserve equality are opposed by the will of the gods, and divine intervention makes unequal what had been equal, gives leadership to one individual among those who are equal.

At the heart of the ancient understanding of democracy is the principle of equality, a denial of a hierarchy among some set of human beings by which we can identify those who ought to have power and authority over others. This, as I see it, is the crux of the ancient perspective on democracy. The sharing of power becomes the answer to the problem of identifying the best ruler in a community of equals. Herodotus expressed the love of equality, constructed or natural, but he does so independently of democracy. He writes mostly of regimes with kings and tyrants, but none of the kings he describes can base his authority only on superiority. They must rely on tricks, on divine prophecies, on uncertain claims of precedence of age. Equality may remain the central value, that which the best laws, like those of the Babylonians concerning marriage, try to construct, but it is also the source of instability when questions of leadership and authority are raised. The political problem is a coherence between equality and order; it is not clear that to Herodotus this problem is resolved by democracy.

V

Book 3 of Herodotus' *Histories* tells of the rise and expansion of Persian power in the East. We learn of Cambyses' invasion of Egypt, of his murder by the pseudo-Smerdis, the Magus who, pretending to be Cambyses' brother, became king. We hear of the seven conspirators who overthrew this pseudo-Smerdis, and finally we hear the famous debate among the conspirators about the best form of government. After the overthrow of the impostor king, no obvious successor emerges—nor is there even any obvious "best regime." The Persian conspirators decide to address the question of which regime is best before they choose who is to rule in that regime.[13] Thus, the seven conspirators "took counsel [*eleubeounto*] about the affairs [*tōn pragmatōn*]" (3.80) and there follow the three speeches which have traditionally and almost universally been referred to as the speeches praising democracy, oligarchy, and monarchy, although the word "democracy" does not appear in the text of any of the speeches.[14]

Otanes gives the first speech, urging that "affairs" be handed over "into the middle" (*es meson*), the same phrase that Maeandrius used when he tried to give up tyrannical power in Samos. Otanes begins his attack on monarchy by asserting that it is not "sweet" (*hēdu*), nor is it "good" (*agathon*), and then assails the unbridled arrogance (*hubris*) of Cambyses, the Magi, and therewith the rule of one man. The bulk of the speech focuses on the impossibility of anyone being a good monarch. Otanes claims that anyone given power becomes arrogant or hubristic and thus will offend the principles of equality. "He does whatever he wishes," Otanes says, using a phrase that we will see recurring later when Aristotle wants to criticize the tyrannical demos in a democracy. Finally, near the conclusion of his speech, Otanes turns to the regime he is praising: "When the many [*plēthos*] is the ruler, first the name is the most beautiful [*kalliston*] of all: *isonomia*, and second, it does none of those things that a monarchy does. It has public office by lot, it has *hupeuthunon* [a trial when one finishes serving in public office], and it brings all deliberations [*bouleumata*] before the community [*en to koinon*]." Thus, Otanes puts his judgment against monarchy and urges that "all things be equal among the many" (3.80).

The passage has called forth generations of admiration with the assurance that Otanes' speech is the intellectual victor, even if it is not the historical one—precisely because we, from our modern perspectives, expect it to be. Donald Kagan, for example, comments: "We must, I believe, reject immediately the possibility that Herodotus supports the argument for monarchy. His love of freedom, dislike of tyranny, the fact that no Greek *polis* was so ruled make this seem certain." Kagan continues: "It is the Athens of Cleisthenes he admires, and it is the Cleisthenic constitution which he sees as the exemplar of liberty and freedom. That constitution was, of course, a popular democratic one. For this reason more than any other it seems proper to identify Herodotus with the praise of democracy voiced by Otanes" (1965, 69–70). More recent readings have noticed the reticence in Otanes' speech. Seth Benardete, for example, comments that Herodotus is silent about what democracy does (1969, 86) and Stewart Flory is even stronger (perhaps too strong) in claiming that the arguments are vague precisely because Otanes (and by implication Herodotus) "apparently cannot think of positive arguments for democracy" (1987, 131).

It is important to attend to the structure of the speech. Flory criticizes it because it focuses almost exclusively on the inherent evils of one-man rule. We are reminded here of Churchill's dictum that democracy is the worst regime except for all the others. As Flory points out, though, the criticisms of one-man rule are contradicted by Herodotus' own *Histories,* filled as the work is with tales of at least as many good monarchs as tyrants. But the issue to which Herodotus, through Otanes, alerts us is precisely that of who is to be ruler, how are we to decide. Otanes catalogues the evils of monarchy and insists that those evils will surface in anyone who has become a superior where once he was an equal. Otanes warns: "Placing even the best of all men [*ton ariston andrōn pantōn*] into such rule you will arouse him outside his accustomed thoughts" (3.80). Monarchy entails inequality and once there is inequality we find outrageousness—the arrogance and the jealousy that bring on the overturning of the ancient customs (*nomaia patria*), the forcing of women, the executions without trial. Inequality leads specifically to the rejection of the *nomoi* that make men equal, even if they are not so by nature.

Disregard of the laws is associated, then, with the denial of an equality that is at the heart of Herodotus' and Athens' values. To place decision-making before all, *es meson*, is not good in itself; it is the mechanism for preventing inequality from leading to the overthrow of the equalizing customs of the city.

In the brief paragraph of Otanes' speech, the word *nomoi* recurs three times. The monarch disregards the *nomoi*, and the beautiful name that Otanes assigns to the regime he praises is *isonomia*. The monarch does whatever he wants because he is unequal or asserts an inequality, claiming not to be bound by laws that bind others. The citizens of an *isonomia* are all equally restrained by the law, whereas a monarchy is lawless. Thus, the two institutional elements to which Herodotus has Otanes point are election by lot, i.e., that which constrains choice since there is no conscious setting of one individual above another; and accountability after completion of office, i.e., no one can do whatever he wants, even when he is in a position of authority. There is thus no opportunity for hubris and the setting up of one to rule over another. Otanes' speech is one praising a political system founded on an equality that has established institutional restraints to resist the negative consequences of the inequalities necessary for leadership in the community.[15]

Megabyzus argues for oligarchy, but he develops this argument by opposing the granting of power to the many. "Than the useless mob," he says, "there is nothing stupider or more arrogant . . . knowledge is not at all in the many." They have no sense of the beautiful. Those who wish the Persians harm should "use the demos." The conspirators should rather join, he suggests, the best of men and rule over Persia (3.81). Megabyzus distinguishes: there are the best of men (*aristoi andres*) and then there are the many (*to plēthos*), the demos, who have not been taught what is beautiful and are unable to recognize it innately. Underlying Megabyzus' claims for oligarchy are innate inequalities of intelligence and the understanding of beauty—arguments that sit uneasily with the rest of Herodotus' *Histories*, at least insofar as they can be used as a principle of political organization.

Darius, the defender of monarchy, speaks last and, while he warns of the conflict (*stasis*) and murders and hatreds that come from both oligarchy and the *dēmos* (a word Darius uses frequently, but one that Otanes, the defender of *isonomia*, avoids), he raises the banner of freedom over that of equality. It is the single man, Cyrus, who freed the Persians (*hēmeas eleutheronteutas dia hēna andra*), and, against the claims of Otanes who attacked monarchy because it failed to preserve the ancestral customs (*patria nomaia*), Darius claims that it is only through monarchy that the Persians will be able to maintain their laws (3.83). He thus finds freedom and lawfulness in monarchy, but obviously makes no claims about equality.

For many reasons, scholars and admirers of Herodotus have focused on this debate as offering the first theoretical defense of democracy. The passages, though, are neither the most charming nor the most profound in a book filled with one wonderful story after another. The importance of the passage, as I see it, does not lie in its supposed defense of democracy, but in the presentation of individuals having to decide where to allocate authority, not on the basis of the qualities of a particular individual, but on an assessment of which institutional arrangements will promote the values of most importance to the speaker. We see here the institutionalization of politics rather than the dependence on personalities. This is the real contribution to democratic theory, not the easily refuted claims about the best being in some abstract middle, *es meson*. It is the capacity of men who, beginning from an equality, are able to share in the process of political choice. That they decide to distribute it to one rather than the many is less important than their awareness that there is a choice to be made equally by those engaged in discussion. We cannot forget, however, that they conclude that security and freedom lie in giving power to one and not to the many, the *plēthos*.

Behind this institutionalization must lie the judgment of what is best for the community as a whole. Justification comes from reason and analysis, not simply preference. Our political institutions, Herodotus tells us, do not spring forth fully grown. The process of choosing, as exemplified in the dramatization of the debate, forces us to articulate the principles behind our regime and to assess those principles. The process of assessment, though, does not lead unambiguously to *isonomia* and the placement of the affairs of the city *es meson*. Indeed, two of the speeches oppose the structure of such a regime, and at least four of the seven conspirators vote to institute a monarchy. The conspirators, presented with the three options, did not see the choice as easy, and Herodotus' *Histories* cannot be read, as Kagan reads it, as a simple brief for any regime. Otanes values a natural equality, but he also recognizes the need to preserve that equality through accountability after service in office. Though all are equal before the law and all are able to hold political office, some may abuse the brief period during which they have power. Equality by nature does not ensure virtue by nature. Megabyzus makes no claims about equality and thus is furthest from the Herodotus we see elsewhere. Megabyzus' concern is that not all men have knowledge of that which is good, a knowledge which must come from teaching and from innate qualities (*oikeion*). Having identified the goal as "the good," Megabyzus presents an easy politics: we simply identify those who have this knowledge and allow them to rule. Darius does not pretend that the answer is so simple and we find him arguing from effects rather than principles or beautiful names. The effect of equality according to Darius is conflict, while the effect of kingship is the freedom that equality, he claims, cannot preserve: "In one word: from what source did we gain our freedom, and who gave it [to] us? The people, or the oligarchy, or the despot? I give my vote that, as we are freed by one man, so we should keep our freedom *through* one man" (3.82, Grene translation). In Darius' version, there is no inherent incompatibility between freedom and monarchy, no identity here between freedom and the placement of the affairs of the city "in the middle."

Throughout, Herodotus is evenhanded in presenting the virtues and defects of regimes. While on the one hand we find the praise of Athenian *isēgoria* and the overthrow of tyranny at Athens which allowed the Athenians to excel over all those around her, we also hear about the susceptibility of the Athenian populace to manipulative speech and tricks. The Athenian populace is persuaded, for instance, by Aristagoras of Miletus to send ships to aid in the Ionian rebellion against the Persians. The Spartan king, Cleomenes, could not be so persuaded (though it was the chance presence of his child that prevented him from being bribed to do so), and Herodotus reflects: "It seems to be easier to trick the many than one; he [Aristagoras] was not able to fool Cleomenes, the sole Lacedaemonian, but he did fool 30,000 Athenians" (5.97). There is also the wonderful story of the trick Peisistratus played in order to return to power in Athens. Having found a tall and beautiful country girl, he dressed her in armor to look like Athena. The people of the city believed that she was the goddess and accepted her command that they receive Peisistratus back from exile (1.60). The regime that puts power in the middle often puts power in the hands of fools, Herodotus seems to be saying, even as it opens doors of greatness to them. Similarly, though, monarchies can be good and they can be bad. For every Cyrus and Amasis, there is a Cambyses and a Xerxes.

Modern readers of the last 150 years seem for the most part to have automatically assumed that Herodotus was praising democracy in the famous debate, but the remaining conspirators supported Darius' views and voted (as equals, we should note) to institute the regime of a monarch. Then it is that they must address the real political challenge and decide how they are to identify the king if they accept the equality that only Megabyzus among them denies. Otanes says: "It is clear that one of us will be king, whether by lot or through selection of the majority of the Persians or in some other fashion" (3.83). Somehow a king (inequality) must be created. As with Amasis, a king is not born, and the artificiality of kingship is perhaps nowhere more obvious than here. The story of how Darius is chosen as the king is revealing. Almost as if using Athenian political inventiveness as their model, a form of lot is decided upon among the conspirators. They make no efforts to discover who is best suited—or, according to Megabyzus' principles, who has the most knowledge, especially of the beautiful. They leave the choice to chance. They will all mount their horses at daybreak and whoever's horse neighs first will become king. It appears to be a system based on chance. Darius' groom, though, was a smart and crafty (*sophos*) man and Darius asks him to devise a trick, which the groom does. On the night before the dawn meeting, the groom brought Darius' stallion to the place where the six were to convene the next morning and allowed the stallion to mount the mare for which he had the most passion. The next morning, when the stallion, with Darius on his back, reached the same spot he had been the night before, he neighed and Darius became king. Some celestial events seemed to support the decision, but what we need to note is that any of the six, or even seven, could have been king; it was the wit of Darius' groom, who knew how to control nature and not leave the selection of the king to chance, that gave Darius the control over Persia. It was not any special qualities that Darius himself possessed. To institute a monarchy, they employ the "democratic" principle of equality.

VI

Throughout his *Histories*, Herodotus focuses our attention on the equality of human beings; he has told us of smart ones and stupid ones, of tall ones and short ones, of men and of women, but none of these differences becomes the basis for the rule of one group or individual over another. The fundamental principle of equality, despite differences, undergirds all of Herodotus' writings and he sees it displayed and flaunted in both East and West. When it is displayed and institutionalized as in *isēgoria* and *isonomia*, it is "beautiful." The political values to which Herodotus turns do not depend on political participation, on the agora active with men seeking immortality through political action. In fact, he often scorns what goes on in the agora and in the institutions that may transform what Jones has called the will of the people into public policy. As the multitude, the demos is not worth much, fooled as it can be by Aristagoras promising an easy victory against the Persians and by a country girl outfitted to look like Athena. But insofar as the regime of Athens *makes* men equal, it follows the best of the customs of the Babylonians, while still leaving open the critical problem of identifying who from that equality should rule.

The praise for freedom we in the modern world have come to associate with democracy has too often made us see in Herodotus only his praise of Athens, while ignoring the other regimes that are free, whether democratic or not. The regime at Athens flourished and had its victories against the Persians not simply because the demos as such rules, but because behind that rule is *isonomia*, where each man works for himself and not for a natural or an artificial master. As we shall see as we progress through our exploration of the ancient Greek response to democracy, it is precisely the issue of equality that is at the core of the philosophers' understanding of democracy; while Herodotus from his *theoria* praises it, we will find that it comes under harsher scrutiny in other authors. But before discussing the philosophers' theorizing about democracy, I turn to Thucydides, who in writing of the democratic city at war does not address equality so much as the consequences, both positive and negative, of the sharing of power.

CHAPTER 3

Thucydides, Communal Decision-Making, and the Capacity for Change

Much has been written on Thucydides and Athenian democracy, most of it similar to the view captured by Thomas Hobbes in the Preface to his translation of Thucydides and quoted already in the first chapter: "For his opinion touching the government of state, it is manifest that he least of all liked the democracy" (1975, 13). Common wisdom often quotes that passage from Book 8 where Thucydides approvingly remarks on the moderate oligarchy of the Five Thousand that was established after the overthrow of the oligarchic Four Hundred. During that period, Thucydides says, the Athenians with a moderate mixture of the few and the many "appear to have carried on well the affairs of the city [*eu politeusante*]" (8.97). I am not here interested in this regime, nor in what is often perceived as Thucydides' aristocratic disdain for the demos.

Rather, I am interested in the way that his history and the speeches that he includes confront the challenge of communal decision-making.[1] Hobbes assumes that Thucydides liked democracy least of all because of the volatility of the demos. This summary of Thucydides' attitude towards democracy is too simple and denies us the opportunity to explore what Thucydides recognizes as foundations of democratic institutions, the benefits of democracy as well as its limits. I argue that it is precisely the potential for political deliberation and the consequent capacity for a city to change policies that characterize the advantages of democracy. In Thucydides' *History* it is when democracies are unable to revoke past decisions that they act in ways harmful to themselves and often offensive to human decency. As the monarchical leader of a democracy, Pericles tries to create an unmoving, disembodied city; but there is also the messy democratic regime of particular bodies, change, and variability, that Thucydides implicitly praises for different qualities. In this chapter I explore how a few speeches in Thucydides' *History* point to how this historian makes us face some of the consequences—both positive and negative—of the Athenians' and others' efforts at communal action through the medium of a democratic assembly.

Pericles' greatest speech in the *History* is without question the Funeral Oration, where he eulogizes the life of the Athenians, their love of beauty without excess, their culture, their resources drawn in by trade, their festivals, their *politeia* that looks to the welfare of the whole, their citizenry who are lovers of the city and who consider the one uninvolved in public life as "useless." This is the speech which, 2,500 years later, could stir the youth of Britain to fight for democracy against the German tyrants. I try here to establish how the Funeral Oration's model of democracy abstracts from history, from particularistic ties, and most especially from bodies. Because of this vision of a city that rises above the past and above bodies, Pericles and the democracy he represents abstract from time, remain unchanging, freed from the past and unrestrained by the demands of the particular. Diodotus in the Mytilenian Debate likewise breaks from the chains of the past to create a new regime, a model of democracy, but one that goes beyond Pericles in its capacity to change by focusing on the future, not on a static moment in time. Pericles' efforts to rise above the past by transforming the city into a unified whole (as with Socrates' Callipolis, the city he founds in speech in the fifth book of the *Republic*) lead to a sterility and vanity that Diodotus' forward-looking regime, which builds on divisions within the city, can avoid. In this sense Diodotus is the real democratic theorist of Thucydides' history, while Pericles appears as his antithesis. Nevertheless, the optimism concerning democracy that we find in the Mytilenian Debate fades when the assemblies that were convened before and during the Sicilian expedition bring divisions to the level of the individual, where they are destructive rather than constructive.

I

Pericles' Funeral Oration is the result of historical precedent, of decisions made in the past that control the present, of the *nomos* that determines what must be done on the occasion of the burial of men who have died for the city in war; but Pericles is critical of this *nomos* that entrusts the deeds of these men to the speech of one man[2] and he is critical of those who have praised this *nomos* from the past (2.35). Pericles expresses respect for the ancestors of the Athenians, but in describing their accomplishments all he notes is that they held onto the land which they inhabited. It is the fathers of those now living who deserve more praise, for they expanded what they received to build the empire; but most of all, it is the men of the present who deserve the greatest praise, for they raised Athens to her current acme of power. The past accomplishments of the ancestors pale before what the present generation has achieved. Pericles sees the past as limiting, to be transcended by the power of the present, and for him it is a present to be preserved, not to be transformed in the future by yet more acquisitions. The Athenians have reached the moment of their greatness; the challenge is to remain there.[3] It is the mistake of later leaders, as Thucydides also notes, driven by the desire for private gain, to try to expand further the perfection of Pericles' city. It is they who bring Athens to defeat (2.65).

By praising Athens this Funeral Oration praises the men who died for Athens; Pericles looks not to individual deeds or accomplishments but to the communal whole. Insofar as the soldiers died in her war, they have become part of, one with, the city, and thus to eulogize the city is to eulogize them. They have no existence independent of the city. Insofar as they are part of this abstract concept, *the city*, they too become abstract, far from their particularized lives where they lived as good or bad men, who loved or beat their wives, cheated or helped their neighbors.[4] As Pericles says: "It is just that manly goodness [*andragathia*] on behalf of a fatherland in war should be set before the failings in other areas; the good public action makes the bad from private action disappear" (2.42.2). As part of this abstraction which is the city, they have died, as Pericles phrases it, "unfelt deaths" (2.43.6), and achieved, through Athens, an eternal fame that depends not on tombstones or markers. Their monuments are found in the uninscribed memory implanted far and wide in the hearts of men. They themselves have become one with Athens; no individuality separates them out from the unified city and no physical monument need recall their deeds.

The city, the abstraction of Athens upon which we feast our eyes in becoming her lovers (*erastes*, 2.43.1), acquires its greatness, though, not from the men who die for her but from the *politeia*, the structure that organizes the various parts of the city. It is, Pericles tells us, a *politeia* that does not imitate the *nomoi*, the laws or customs, of her neighbors, but is a *paradeigma* to be copied by others (2.37.1). In language obscure even to the well-trained Greek scholar, Pericles describes the qualities of this regime. It is here that the word *dēmokratia* appears and the explanation is given that it is called such because it "looks after" (*oikein*) the many rather than the few (2.37.1). Further, the laws give an equality (*to ison*) to each citizen despite private differences (*idia diaphora*), but it is a strange kind of equality, for it emphatically does not lead to equality among all citizens who attend the assembly and make judgments in the courts. Rather, it dismisses "heritage" or "class" (*meros*) as the basis for inequality, and replaces it with a new basis for inequality, namely, virtue. Worth, not wealth (i.e., the relationship to land and property—or to history), determines esteem. In extolling the new democratic world, Pericles makes clear how democracy entails an abstraction from history, from the past, from the old bases of inequality grounded in the experiences of individuals and of the family. The new democratic hierarchy sets Pericles on top, not because of his family connections, not because of his ties to a particular portion of land, but because, independent of all that, he has "virtue," the capacity to serve the common good. Family connections fade into obscurity in the context of the democratic city, just as they did as the result of Cleisthenes' reforms which broke the patriarchal tribes into abstract administrative units. But that does not mean the end of hierarchy.[5]

Pericles goes on: "Freely, we live as citizens, freely both towards that which is commonly shared and towards one another in our daily affairs" (2.37.2). This lack of restraint, though, he assures us, does not lead to lawlessness. On account of fear, the Athenians obey those in authority as well as the laws. And of the laws, we learn, the most important are the ones unwritten, i.e., known only by the mind, which bring shame to the transgressor. Such is the *politeia* for which the men of Athens fought and died. Pericles follows this with a discourse on military style which likewise abstracts from bodies. He does not talk of training bodies or fashioning arms but instead discusses the Athenian policy of openness, while we learn that the military achievements of the Athenians lie less in the traditional armaments of war (*paraskeuais*) than in the unseen, interior "good soul" (*eupsuchē*, 2.39.1).[6]

Pericles admits that there are some among the Athenians concerned with private household affairs and others with the affairs of the city, but when the former turn toward their labor, there is no lack of political concern, nor, he claims, do the Athenians think that reason and speech are a hindrance to action; rather, reason and speech are essential to acting well. Implicit in this paragraph (2.40) is the *ecclēsia*, the assembly, with its deliberative role before decisions are made by the city, but absent is any explicit mention of the institution which, with the courts, is at the core of Athenian democracy. The regime of Athens as it appears in Pericles' speech seems as devoid of political institutions as its soldiers are of bodies, though it is, of course, the institutions that enable Athens to function under Pericles' leadership and it is the bodies, which very much felt their death, that enabled her soldiers to fight.

As others have noted, we are reminded of this abstraction from bodies almost immediately in Thucydides' description of the plague that befell Athens with particularly harsh effect, since during wartime all the Athenians were gathered within the city walls. As Thucydides describes the plague, he writes of the fevers and the chills, the boils and the nausea, the thirst and the ineffectual retching. We leave behind Pericles' speech where death is unfelt and where we can abstract from our bodies to become *erastes* of the city, as if the abstract city can have erotic lovers, as if eroticism did not in some way involve the body. We move from that bodiless world of the Funeral Oration to one almost exclusively of human bodies, deteriorating, dying, festering, or burning on the many funeral pyres throughout the city. The city of Athens, located in place and time, inhabited by citizens with human bodies, organized in certain ways to develop policy outcomes, cannot dissociate the mind and the body as does Thucydides in his descriptions of speech in the Funeral Oration, on the one hand, and of deed in the reporting of the plague, on the other. In the description of the plague, we find Thucydides regrettably showing that the communal life of discourse, where no deed is too daring to be imagined and then attempted, must yield to the bodies of men who die, be it by sickness or by a spear in battle. It is not a pretty picture of these bodies, but it is one that brings us down from the mental, abstract world of the Funeral Oration.

Nevertheless, the Funeral Oration with its disembodiment gives us the foundation for the Pericles we see in his other speeches, the Pericles who can resist the changes demanded by bodies enmeshed in the physical world. Bodies are subject to change, but the mind of Pericles, abstracted from history and abstracted from particularity, can—and does—remain the same. He begins, for example, his first speech in Book 1: "I have always the same mind [gnōmē]—not to yield to the Peloponnesians" (1.140). Others, he notes, do not retain the same passion (orgē) and when circumstances change, they change their minds. Pericles gives the same counsel as he gave before and warns the Athenians that when the war starts and when their circumstances change, they too must resist the temptation to lessen their resolve.

To "remain the same," though, he removes himself from the details of an embodied life. While he describes the resources and skills the Athenians have, the naval power and the tribute from their "allies" in particular, he also urges the Athenians to go to war by telling his fellow citizens to cast off thoughts of land and household, gē and oikia, which tie them to particularities of place and person. Consider this, he tells them: "If we were an island, we would be less susceptible to being seized" (1.143). The Athenians, thinking of themselves as an island, will be able to win the war. The Athenians through their minds must break the ties to their physical being, their physical possessions, and the geographic specifics of their city. Pericles' speeches give to the mind an amazing potential—the apparent power to transform the physical world on its own. In recalling the deeds of "our fathers" against the Medes, he reminds them that it was "mind" (gnōmē) more than any "daring" and more than power (dunamis) that enabled them to save themselves from the Persians. But this power of the mind is only apparent. Athens is not an island and people cannot give up all thought of *gē* and *oikia*. Indeed, this is precisely why Pericles must give his third speech.

After the second invasion by the Spartans and the devastation of the plague, Thucydides presents a city shattered, where lawlessness prevails and where men now openly dare to do what previously they had done only in private. The beauty of the city, the ability of fear to ensure obedience to the laws, the love of the city, all these have faded and the Spartans continue to ravage the plains outside the walls of the city. Now, as Thucydides phrases it, "The Athenians had changed their minds [*elloionto*[7] *tas gnōmas*] and blamed Pericles for convincing them to go to war and that on account of him they had fallen on other misfortunes" (2.59). Thucydides does not explain how the Athenians "changed their minds," though the change must have led to a decision in the assembly to send ambassadors on a failed mission to plead for peace (2.59).[8] In response to this loss of spirit among his fellow citizens and their consequent change of mind, Pericles called a *sullogon*—a talking together.[9]

From this *sullogon* (which he refers to as an *ecclēsia* in the actual speech) we hear only the speech by Pericles, his third—and last—in Thucydides' text. We do not know if others spoke against him. Pericles now confronts most directly the challenge of the democratic regime, a challenge that he had wanted to avoid: the tension between the citizen as mind and the citizen as body, between the citizen who can abstract from the changes that events, circumstances, history bring to bodily well-being and the citizen who feels directly war's effects on the life he lives. The fanciful image of a city on which we gaze as *erastes*, in which the laws provide an equality to all in their private differences, and which is transformed into an island by the mind, yields to a city in which men and women do care about and love their own families, their own land, their own property, where they must face the challenge of preserving themselves, where their *eros* is directed towards that which is private rather than public, where they weep at the loss of fathers, sons, brothers, and husbands, and where all these traumas divide what was a unified city. The devastation of their land when the Lacedaemonians invaded confirms that they are not an island, however much they make it so in their minds, and the devastation of their bodies from the plague confirms how much chance affects them, however much they may try to rise above it.

The plague, the invasion, the plundering of their land, the suffering rather than the promised easy victory left the Athenians wondering about the wisdom of the policy to which Pericles had previously persuaded them and for which they had voted. Pericles now must persuade them to resist their doubts and maintain the "same mind" that they had when they first supported him in their decision to stand firm and face the prospect of war rather than yield to the demands of the Spartans. Pericles' third speech to the discontented Athenians is to acknowledge the limits that bodies place on the mind, and it offers a far less glorious view of the city and what it can accomplish, while still insisting that the Athenians remain firm in their resolve, that they do not change.

In his first speech, Pericles had urged the Athenians not to yield to the Lacedaemonians. Now they must not yield (*eikete*) to their sufferings (2.60; cf. 1.141). Pericles must turn them away from their private experiences toward that which is shared, the city in its great abstraction that he had so praised in the Funeral Oration. He even becomes a bit petulant as he describes how they, the Athenians, have changed their minds. They should not change. He remains the same as he was before. Why do they now unfairly attack him? We know why: they blame him because events and experiences have indeed altered them, because the world of bodies does not remain the same. What was persuasive before no longer persuades when experience undermines expectations. Recalling the language of the first speech, Pericles in his third speech now says to those assembled: "I am myself and I do not move. You alter [*metaballete*]" (2.61). Words that once convinced them "no longer appear correct because of the weakness of your mind [gnōmē]" (2.61). Pericles complains that misfortunes at home (kat' oikon) have beaten them down and thus they cast off the safety of the whole, the koinon (2.60). They do not remain firm in what they knew or agreed to (zunegnōte, 2.60).[10] Using a loaded word, Pericles now accuses them of having become enslaved (douloi) by their unexpected physical sufferings. He urges them to rise above their grief at their private losses and not diminish their fame. They must transcend their history, what they own, those whom they love. Again recalling his first speech, where he told them to cast off thoughts of gē and oikia, he says here that they should consider "the use of household and land [ton oikion kai tēs gēs] mere adornments [enkallopisma], like gardens, and worth little" (2.62). Only by ignoring their private experiences that relate to the physical world they experience directly will they ensure freedom rather than subservience to others.

But Pericles must go beyond simply making them forget their private suffering; he must draw them back into one coherent whole again. Attention to body and to what is private divides; it makes us aware of what separates, not what unites us with our fellow citizens. It is only by casting off attachments to bodies that we can unite the city into one—and, as one, make the city have one mind, not many minds. When Pericles encourages his listeners to dismiss thoughts of the mere embellishments of land and household, he foreshadows Socrates in the *Republic*, who takes away from his warriors and later his philosopher rulers all that is *oikeion*, private: homes, land, wives, and children—anything that might mark them as separate from their fellow citizens. Pericles does not go quite so far in deed as Socrates does in his speech, but in his exhortations to the Athenians to dismiss the private as mere embellishments (and earlier to become *erastes* of the city), he too is trying to build a unified city. Socrates in the *Republic*, aiming to unify his city, proposes that it will be so much a community of pain and pleasure that when one of its members cuts his or her finger, everyone will say "ouch" (462c). The image, of course, is absurd, and I (as do others) would argue that this raises questions about whether Socrates is being serious in the founding of this city,[11] but at the same time it is meant to show the beauty of a city that can act as if it were a unified whole, one body rather than a conglomeration of separate, individual bodies. The experiences of the war with Sparta, however, had turned the Athenian citizens toward their own travails, had separated them from others so that the city of one unchanging mind under the spell of Pericles had become divided into many minds. Can a community be re-created out of those individual sufferings?

The Athenian *politeia* so praised by Pericles entails the participation and involvement of each citizen; in so doing, however, it brings to the core of the decision-making process individual members with their own suffering and their own lands and households. As such, there will be variability in their decisions and a weaving back and forth. The city that Pericles envisaged in the Funeral Oration contradicts the engagement entailed in the activity of democratic decision-making that he so praised. The variety of experiences of embodied citizens who acknowledge the demands of their bodies and their particular attachments that come from those bodies creates divergent interests. The unexpected suffering that the war has brought divides the city into individuals who care about their private welfare, who are no longer *erastes* of the city, who see themselves as private rather than communal beings, who do not accept the Funeral Oration's identification between themselves and the city. The uniformity that precludes changes cannot be modeled onto the city of Athens made up of a multiplicity of men who experience pain and who, as the result of sufferings very much felt, do not accept the identification of themselves with Athens.[12]

Pericles standing before the Athenians, asserting his imperviousness to change, strives to make the assembly and the city one, like an individual. That was his goal in the Funeral Oration—to identify so closely the city with the individual that individual citizens did not see themselves as distinct, as having identifiable personalities apart from the city. That is why the image of *erastes* is so important, suggesting the merging into one rather than the preservation of the many; that is why the dead need no monuments, why the parents, sons, wives need not weep. The plague, though, indicated the vanity of such a goal. Thus, Pericles' third speech, like the Funeral Oration, strives to re-create (or really invent) the decision-making body as one and unified, just as the city itself must be one.

Thucydides' reporting of Pericles' speeches allows Pericles to speak each time without an opponent. Pericles does not draw out the divisions in the assembly because he presents the city as a whole, as a mental construct abstracted from particularities. In contrast, democracy as a regime where individuals rule and control themselves, where they debate alternatives, a regime which is not simply *administered* for the sake of the many, depends on the multiplicity of views that derives from a multiplicity of experiences, not on the unity of the *homilos*. In Thucydides' Periclean democracy, we hear only one view forcefully presented, the one that moves the whole, the one that tries to make men bodiless. But, of course, an assembly is not a person; it can never have one mind. The assembly is a constantly fluctuating conglomeration of particular individuals. Those who voted for the war may not be the same as those who now view peace as the better option and vote to send ambassadors to the Lacedaemonians. When Pericles accuses those who sit in the assembly, saying to them: "You change [*metaballete*] . . . the incorrectness of my mind [my wisdom, opinion] lies in your own weakness," this need not refer to the weakness of the individual attendees at the assembly as Pericles would suggest; it is a "weakness" of a regime where decisions are made by parts as if they were the whole. Pericles as one, as an individual, can provide steadfastness; he can remain himself.

The assembly cannot provide such steadfastness since, unlike the person of Pericles, it is not one. It cannot be one because it is made up of many bodies. Pericles, whose rhetoric abstracts the individual from his body, cannot do the same in deed and so the city comprised of many individuals alters and does not remain the same.

Thucydides' summary of the events that follow the third speech of Pericles captures the tension well. As a people, *dēmosia*, the Athenians were persuaded. Insofar as they were able to be united into a whole, they remained the same and did not sue for peace; but in private they continued to grieve over their separate differences, and we even find here Thucydides making distinctions between the people, *ho dēmos*, who were deprived of whatever little they had and the powerful, *hoi dunatoi*, who grieved over the loss of their beautiful possessions (2.65.2). These are distinctions which cannot be allowed in the unified assembly that is beyond conflict. It is at this point that Thucydides offers his famous assessment of Pericles' career and his explanation of why the Athenians lost the war; what is of most interest for my purposes, though, is the reappearance of the word *dēmokratia*. Thucydides summarizes: "In speech [*logōi*] it was a democracy, in deed [*ergōi*] it was the rule of one man" (2.65.9). The distinction holds insofar as the assembly was divided, individuated, and thus unable to remain itself. Insofar as Pericles could unify the citizens in their love for the city and their identification with what was common rather than what was private, the democratic regime was no different than the rule of one man. Insofar as an assembly was uniform and could achieve such a clear vision of how the city might act, there would be no need for debate and discourse. For the most part, though, assemblies cannot reach the uniformity of one man, even under the spell of Periclean rhetoric, and so they debate and, even more significantly, they change their minds and yield to new sentiments and new arguments.

In contrast to the Periclean speeches stands the Mytilenian Debate. There we see how communal decision-making among differing self-interested individuals may lead to better policy outcomes, even if it means that the assembly (and the people within it) change their minds, an eventuality that Pericles, encouraging steadfastness, discourages. The Mytilenian Debate is between Cleon, whom Thucydides calls the most violent of men, and Diodotus, an otherwise unknown character whose name means the "gift of Zeus" and whose patronymic, Eucrates, means "good rule." With such an introduction to both characters Thucydides' own preferences are evident. These two speakers debate whether the assembly should revoke a policy decision it voted on the day before, when Cleon's views had been victorious (*enenikēkei*, 3.36.6). Thucydides does not record the speeches that led to the original decision. The debate we do hear is whether the Athenians should remain firm, not change their previous decision, or whether they should relent because of the harshness of the earlier decree and vote differently this time. The decision under discussion has to do with the punishment decreed for the Mytilenians who, though subject to the Athenians, had refused to send money to them, as the Athenians required of their "allies." The Athenians easily put down the rebellion, but were left with the question of how to punish the rebel city. "Under the influence of anger," Thucydides reports, "it seemed best to the Athenians to kill not only those who had participated, but also all the adult male population and to sell the women and children into slavery" (3.36).

The decision came from the passions of the moment, but the next day there was "a certain change of mind [*metanoia tis*] and a re-calculation [*analogismos*] about how great was the decision to destroy the whole city rather than those who were responsible" (3.36). In other words, they question whether they should treat the city of Mytilene as if it were a unified whole rather than made up of multiple parts. The Mytilenian ambassadors and their Athenian supporters arrange for the decision to come before the assembly again. Thucydides comments that this was not difficult since most of the citizens wished that someone would give them the opportunity to deliberate on their decision again. It is in this context that we have the debate between Cleon, who urges the Athenians to persevere in the previous decision to punish all, and Diodotus, who asks the Athenians, for the sake of expediency, to change their minds and revoke the previous decree, punishing only those who were responsible for the rebellion.

The curious echoes of Pericles' words and stance in Cleon's speech have been noted before, but usually with attention to how the two speeches are slightly different.[13] I would suggest that the focus on the differences arises because of the tendency of contemporary authors to lionize Pericles and to pick up Thucydides' hostility towards Cleon. But Pericles is in many ways preparatory for the Cleon of the Mytilenian Debate. The differences between Cleon and Pericles appear most notably in Pericles' qualification when he tells the Athenians: "Your empire is like a tyranny" (2.63.2), whereas the violent Cleon bluntly says: "Your empire is a tyranny" (3.37.2). But to concentrate on this distinction blinds us to the way in which we must see Cleon as the consequence of Pericles, carrying out the Periclean vision of the Athenian regime to its extreme, as an unchanging uniformity that remains itself.

Cleon begins his own speech: "Often have I thought that it is impossible for a *dēmokratia* to rule over others" (3.37). Pericles, Thucydides tells us, in transforming Athens into a monarchy in deed, made Athens capable of ruling over others. It was under Pericles as a democratic leader that the empire of Athens grew, but it was also Pericles who defined the *dēmokratia* of Athens as a *politeia* that governs in the interest of the many, not as a regime that places authority, to use the language from Herodotus, *en meson*. It was Pericles who urged the Athenians to become unified and unchanging in their views, firm in their convictions. It is

Cleon who now says to the Athenians: "The most dreadful thing of all is that our decisions are not firm or secure nor do we know that the city using laws that are bad but unmoving [*akinētois*] is stronger than the one using good laws that lack authority" (3.37.3). Here he sounds like the Spartan Archidamus of Book 1, who had argued that Spartan success rested on the unwillingness to challenge laws already in place (1.84.3). Cleon appears un-Athenian in this predilection for permanence[14]—but, again, so did Pericles when he followed (at the same time as finding fault with) the law commanding funeral orations, and when he urged the Athenians to be unmoving in their convictions.[15]

Cleon desires permanence, decisiveness, commitment, none of which characterize a deliberative body of decision makers. Pericles worried about individuals divided from the common purpose because of their personal suffering, but his goal was the same, to make the citizen body one, strong in its previous decisions, impervious to change. Cleon rails against the cleverness of those who debate, who engage in bandying ideas and arguments about, and against citizens who set up contests of words which resemble theater productions. Thus, citizens lose conviction about what has been thoroughly examined and approved. They become slaves of novelty and scornful of the customary. In contrast, Cleon remains himself. Echoing Pericles, he says: "I myself am the same in my mind" (3.38.1). He does not want wasteful deliberation that leads to the pursuit of novelty rather than the preservation of what already is. Pericles certainly does praise the Athenians for not regarding words as a hindrance to deeds and for recognizing that speech is preparatory to action (2.40.2); from Cleon there is no praise for speeches nor for debate and deliberation. In Cleon's view the city that allows for the practice of oratory submits itself to constant transformations, precisely what Pericles fears as well. Stability is what is needed and stability arises from a unity and uniformity, a refusal to build on divisions within the city. We might note that Cleon also wants to see Mytilene as a whole. Punish the *whole* city as if it were one, he tells the Athenians. "Let not the blame rest on the few [*hoi oligoi*], while you release the demos" (3.39.6). All alike set against the Athenians and thus all alike deserve punishment.[16]

Thucydides' attitude toward Cleon has been widely accepted: Thucydides scorns him and puts him in the worst light possible,[17] but to so describe Thucydides' views on Cleon leaves us wrestling with Thucydides' attitude to Pericles and the ways in which Pericles' vision of Athens foreshadows the antidemocratic Cleon—and indeed an antidemocratic Athens. If this is reprehensible in Cleon, why not in Pericles? Does Pericles' view of the unified city give us a false beauty that becomes ugly once articulated by a character like Cleon?

Cleon's speech, filled with the anger of the injured, demands justice. It is perhaps the introduction of concepts of justice that makes the dangers of his desires for a static regime the most threatening. If we think back to the original meaning of justice as the preservation of the status quo, the return to what was a previous distribution, we can get a good sense of how Cleon with his claim for justice looks to the preservation of what was rather than a consideration of what will be—or the necessity of change. Like Pericles, he wishes to pursue a moment in time and to do so he must ignore (or diminish) the role of the assembly of embodied citizens.

Diodotus, coming forward to urge change, is, I suggest, the true democratic theorist from antiquity and he is, I suspect, entirely the product of Thucydides' imagination. While Thucydides without hesitation puts arguments and ideas, that which is necessary (*ta deonta*, 1.22), into the speech of others throughout his *History*, Diodotus as his creation speaks what Thucydides thinks is necessary. In this speech Diodotus reminds us that the deliberative body is not one, a unified person that moves uniformly through time and space. He himself had argued against the harsh decree previously and now urges the Athenians not to remain the same, to be willing to change, not to remain themselves, but to do what deliberative bodies will do, recognize the complexity of decisions. This may mean changing. Diodotus translates this principle to communal decision-making. Like Pericles, Diodotus does not want to be bound by history; his is a perspective that looks forward. Cleon's concept of justice had been backward looking. It was a justice of revenge, a justice that demanded that the evil deeds of the past not be forgotten simply because they were past.[18] Retribution must be exacted from those who have caused pain. Thus, Mytilene must suffer. Diodotus, the gift of the gods, says we must look forward; justice is worthless if it only looks backward and tries to reestablish an ancient order, to preserve what has been. Diodotus asks the Athenians to focus on what will be; they must not be restrained by past orders or stances, by what was, but by what will serve the interests of Athens in the future. Diodotus' justice, like democracy, must be able to lift itself out of history and address what will be rather than what has been.

Thus his speech begins by noticing that he, in contrast to Cleon, does not blame those who have brought forth consideration of the decree again, nor does he find fault with the frequent reconsideration of the most important matters. He does not want a unified, static assembly that cannot change itself; he wants one where there are open divisions of opinion. In particular, against the implications in Cleon's speech that the speakers in the assembly come forth only for personal gain, Diodotus insists that such calumny threatens the open discourse of varied opinions that must confront an unclear future (*tou mellontos . . . mē emphanous*, 3.42.2). All must speak without fear of losing their reputations for honesty or else the city will lose the benefits of speakers who reflect honestly on the alternatives. It is necessary, says Diodotus, that the good citizen argue with good reasons and not win by fear, while the wise city causes no loss in reputation to the advisers whose counsel is not followed. Only thus will speakers speak from conviction and reason and not with a view to the passions of the many or for personal gain. Diodotus argues for argument, for debate, for divisions, for a multiplicity of perceptions which are drawn into assessments of what actions the city should take. He does not ask that they agree, only that they not speak from self-interest or the desire to flatter. The threat is not of divisions within the city concerning the opinions of what ought to be done, but that the speakers might not speak with a view towards what they consider best for the city rather than for themselves.

With this as a preface, Diodotus turns to his argument from expediency. The Athenians misconstrue the role of punishment if they see it only in terms of revenge, of what is due, of what is just, of the attempt to reestablish a previous norm; they must consider it in terms of what effect it will have on preventing future rebellions and expenditures of resources. Thus, in this first set of paired Athenian speeches we see the deliberative body at odds with itself, we see it divided in opinions and not remaining firm as Pericles (and Cleon) had urged. We see the democratic system of debate and *isēgoria* defended in the second speech by the man to whom Thucydides gives the name "the gift of Zeus, son of good power."

When Diodotus is through speaking, Thucydides acknowledges that the views most opposed to each other had been spoken and that the Athenians came into the contest almost the same in opinion; at the counting of hands, they were nearly equally divided. But the view of Diodotus won, and, by chance, the ship sent to stay the previous day's decree met no contrary winds and thus was able to stop what Thucydides calls in one of the few openly evaluative comments of the work the "monstrous [*allokoton*]" deed (3.49.4). The image of the second ship chasing after the first ship vividly portrays a city divided within itself, a city that did not remain firm in its convictions, a city that yielded to a change of feeling and opinion and because of its capacity to change performed the noble deed, not the vicious retributive acts of the violent Cleon. Had Cleon's or Pericles' invocations to their fellow citizens to remain firm in their minds been heeded, all the adult males of Mytilene would have been executed and the women and children sold into slavery. The democracy, not the rule of one man, or the city unified in itself as Pericles envisioned, prevented the monstrous deed. The democracy debating within itself, not whole, not complete, not uniform, prevents horrendous deeds. The city that moves, that does not remain still in a bodiless moment in time, punishes only a part because it can recognize the multiplicity of bodies that comprise a city; this city enables Thucydides to sigh his sigh of relief that the innocent were spared the harshest of punishments.

It is the assembly of embodied men who debate and bring to the debate their individual experiences, not the disembodied lovers of the beautiful city who listen only to Periclean speeches. I see here a Thucydides not "least of all liking democracy," but a Thucydides concerned about the democracy of the preeminent man that abstracts from the bodies of the everyday pleasures of the human being, the pleasures of the house and of the garden; a Thucydides not condemning but praising the variability of a democracy; a Thucydides who acknowledges the benefits that emerge from constant reassessments based on an understanding such as Diodotus has of what happened before.

Thucydides writes a work to be a possession forever (*ktēma es aiei*, 1.22), but this does not mean that his readers must be bound by and limited by what has happened in the past, as Cleon was, but that the readers, seeing clearly (*saphes skopein*, 1.22), can look forward and acknowledge the necessity for change when their experiences demand it. My reading of the Mytilenian Debate suggests that what intrigues Thucydides about the Athenian assembly is that it becomes a protection against certainty. Pericles as a single ruler could not reassess decisions, and he asks his city not to do so either. Democracy's advantage—not its disadvantage—is that it can change, that it is not captured by its history or by any moment in time. In this way, it is the democratic regime that can benefit from the Thucydidean endeavor to enable men to "see clearly" (1.22.4). If all were to be bound by what was, if all were committed to preserving what is, there would be no need for the work of Thucydides.

III

In Books 6 and 7 of his *History* Thucydides paints a more ambivalent picture of the possibilities of communal decision-making than we find in Diodotus' speech. These are the books in which Thucydides describes the decision to invade Sicily and the disasters for Athens that followed that decision. While the process of debate, division, and opposing views may lead to more humane acts, as in the refusal to carry out the first decree against the inhabitants of Mytilene, the deliberative process of the assembly does not protect Athens from the divisions surrounding the far more destructive expedition to Sicily. In Books 6 and 7 we see the dangers of a failure to reassess and to change rather than the success of the ship that, sailing quickly, prevented the most horrendous of deeds. Let us go very briefly through some of the speeches that mark the decision-making process at this junction in the *History* and see how they play out in the decisions of democratic assemblies.

After many victories and losses and several years of peace, the Athenians, attracted by the reported wealth of Sicily, voted to send sixty ships to Sicily with Alcibiades, Nicias, and Lamachos as generals. Thucydides does not record the debates about whether to go on this expedition, but on the fifth day after the first vote was taken, the *ecclēsia* met again to decide how to furnish the ships as quickly as possible. Nicias, who had opposed the expedition in the first meeting, tries in un-Periclean fashion (but in Diodotean fashion) to convince the Athenians to change their minds, to turn away from their previous decision. He begins by recognizing that the *ecclēsia* has been called to consider preparations for the invasion, but he uses the opportunity to raise again the question of the invasion. As with Diodotus, all must be open to debate and reassessment, to argument and analysis. This is best for the city. As Diodotus explained, a democratic regime depends on *isēgoria* and the opportunity to express openly what one thinks, and Nicias does so now. He tells the Athenians that they have come to their decisions about the greatest things too quickly. Though he recognizes the honor for him personally in the expedition, "not previously for the sake of honor have I spoken contrary to my mind [*gnōmē*] nor now, but what I know is best I will say" (6.9.2).

Accepting Diodotus' premise that the wise regime must not dismiss an opinion honestly expressed, Nicias presents his concerns about the proposed expedition, the enemies left behind, the Sicily which would be difficult to rule even were the Athenians to conquer her, the self-seeking Athenians (in particular, Alcibiades) who want this expedition for personal glory and not the welfare of the city. He concludes by asking the Prytanes, the men who control the agenda of the *ecclēsia*, to allow the Athenians to vote again, to show that the city is not uniform and intransigent, but of divided opinions and capable of change. The debate sought by Nicias did occur, but most still favored the expedition and opposed "undoing what had been voted [*epsēphismena*], though some spoke against it" (6.15.1). Had the Athenians indeed changed their minds and undone their previous vote, they would have spared themselves much suffering.[19] The assembly opened the possibility of change, but it was an opportunity lost.

It is in Alcibiades' speech, though, that we see the dangers of the equal opportunity to speak, for it allows Alcibiades to bring to the deliberations discourse about himself rather than about public policy. Though Cleon may have been violent, though he may have been wrongheaded in his conception of justice, though his speech may have attacked the principles of democracy, he spoke about public policy. Alcibiades begins with himself: "It is fitting for me more than others to rule and I think I am worthy of it" (6.16.1). Though others like Pericles and Diodotus and Nicias had stressed the individual's dependence on the well-being of the city, Alcibiades suggests that the city's well-being depends on him, on his achievements as a private individual that set him apart from an equality with others. He brings individuality into the debate; Pericles had proposed unity, a unity that came from abstraction from the land, from all being lovers of the city, from the absence of disagreement. Diodotus encouraged divisions as the best mechanism for discovering the best opinions from the city's many councilors. Alcibiades introduces himself as being superior to others because of his reputation and successes in the games at Olympia. The Athenians to whom the speeches are given in order to influence their votes are drawn in by the personality of Alcibiades, as their love for Alcibiades—and for the expedition (6.24.3)—replaces the love Pericles had sought for the abstract city. And so the Athenians voted straightaway for the expedition, not heeding Nicias' advice to change their vote, to reassess, and to be variable. Eros intrudes here as it did in Pericles' Funeral Oration, uniting the city but also making it incapable of changing the previous decision to set forth on the doomed expedition.

News of the impending expedition reaches Syracuse, where we find, as in Athens, men deliberating about the actions that are to be taken by the community as a whole. Thucydides reports these deliberations in which we again confront the question of divisions and unity in a democratic society. Hermocrates speaks first in the *ecclēsia* of the Syracusans, and the openness of the discourse that Diodotus had demanded for his city is apparent in this speech. Recognizing that men speaking in the assembly are often thought to be fools, Hermocrates nevertheless will not restrain himself when the city is in danger (6.33.1). There follow in his speech precise calculations about how best to deal with the impending invasion. The rhetoric is sparse, the policy recommendations careful, namely, to acknowledge the threat and to act on it. He warns the Syracusans that they must not yield to their "customary quiet [*to zunēthes hēsuchon*]" (6.34.4), i.e., they must not remain still and unchanging.

Following the report of Hermocrates' speech, Thucydides notes that the Syracusan demos was in great strife against one another (*pollēi . . . eridi*, 6.35.1). It is in this context that Athenagoras, "the leader of the demos and at the time the most believed by the many" (6.35.2), spoke in opposition to Hermocrates and tried to unify and calm the city by viciously attacking him. As Alcibiades' speech had focused on himself as an individual whose personal greatness elevated the city, so Athenagoras focuses on Hermocrates as an individual whose deviousness would undermine the strength of the city. Having private fears, such men as Hermocrates wish to put the city into its disturbances so that they can conceal their own fears in a common fright (6.36.2). Athenagoras bases his own dismissal of Hermocrates' claims on the assumed rationality of the Athenians—skillful and experienced men who would never leave the Peloponnese before the war is securely finished. In other words, he himself speaking to the assembled Syracusans does not acknowledge how assemblies of the sort to which he now speaks can vote policies that are not wise in their consequences or in the interest of the community as a whole— though he himself is about to make one of the most divisive speeches in the whole *History*. Had the Greeks used Latin, Athenagoras' speech could only be described as an *ad hominem* tirade.

To complement this tirade, Athenagoras launches into what may be the most sustained and important claims concerning democracy in Thucydides' *History*. Against the arguments of some that "by nature" a *dēmokratia* is not wise (*zuneton*) or equal (*ison*) and that therefore those with wealth ought to rule, he argues: "But I say that the demos is the name of the whole, while oligarchy is the name of a part. . . . and that the many are the best suited, having listened to debates, to make judgments and that all these things individually and all together are equally shared in a democracy" (6.39.1). Like Pericles, Athenagoras wants to emphasize the wholeness of the city. It is men like Hermocrates, bringing their unique advice into the assembly, who divide the city. Having praised the community, the equality, the rightness of a democracy, Athenagoras turns to a vicious attack on the self-interested motives of the most foolish, most lacking in learning, most unjust men in all of Greece, who bring forth false warnings only to get power for themselves. Concluding with the rhetoric of slavery and freedom, he urges the assembled Syracusans to dismiss the threats that Hermocrates has made and to reject those who have brought them forth for their own self-advancement.

As if to underscore the *ad hominem* nature of the debate he has just described, Thucydides has an unnamed general rise and stop further debate with the admonition that it is not moderate (*sōphron*) for some to speak accusations against one another or for listeners to hear such things (6.41.1). Seeming to follow Hermocrates instead of Athenagoras, this unnamed general urges that they as individuals and the city as a whole might best prepare to repel those who may be coming against them. After this unnamed general reminds the Syracusans of the need for unity rather than divisive calumnies, the Syracusans depart from the assembly. Thucydides records no vote, but the events—the arrival of the Athenians at Sicily and the ensuing battle—confirm Hermocrates' predictions, he who urged that the Syracusans act rather than remain their static selves. The Syracusans appoint generals with full powers, as Hermocrates subsequently proposes, with no opposing speech reported by Thucydides. The immediacy of the crisis leaves little time for debate.

The challenges of communal decision-making are perhaps nowhere more poignantly visible than in the Athenian camp outside Syracuse prior to the disastrous defeat of the Athenians. Demosthenes, the general who has replaced Alcibiades, proposes retreat; Nicias proposes otherwise—precisely because he claims to know the "nature of the Athenians" (7.48.4)—or the inadequacies of the assembly at Athens, where those who will vote on their actions will rely on those who speak their accusations well, but will pay little attention to what had really been the case. Even many of the soldiers, indeed most of them, on their return to Athens, would not speak truthfully about what had happened in Sicily, blaming the generals for yielding to bribes and retreating against the wishes of the soldiers themselves. Thus, Nicias remains determined to stay despite the inclination of the two other generals to leave. The Athenians do remain; they are surrounded and, despite a powerful exhortation by Nicias, they succumb after a chaotic battle, leaving many of their wounded to die there on the battlefield and the survivors to die later as slaves in the salt mines.

Had Nicias believed in the viability of the democratic processes of decision-making, had he believed that observation and truth would win out over fancy and accusation, had he not known the power of good speech whether well-founded or not, had he thought that the assembly would change its mind, he might have been willing to return to Athens defeated, but prepared to explain why. But he knew too well the nature of the deliberative process and so he stayed, convinced the others to stay, and died, as Thucydides says, "least worthy of his misfortune" (7.86.5). Here certainly, the optimism about debate, divisions, and changeability apparent in the Mytilenian Debate is long gone. Nicias no longer shows any faith in democratic deliberation. Neither we nor Thucydides, however, can know whether the speculations of Nicias about the functioning of the assembly were correct. Because of his insistence that the troops remain in Sicily, we are never given the opportunity to learn.

IV

This is indeed a bare sketch of some of the places in his *History* where Thucydides (as a theorist of far more than relations between cities) confronts the nature of democratic institutions. His *History* presents us with ancient democracy as a challenge of decision-making by a group of citizens deliberating about public policy. The issues of equality seldom surface in this discussion, except, for example, in Athenagoras' demagogic accusations against the supposed threat of the well-to-do for the welfare of Syracuse. Rather, the concern is far more often with the degree to which citizens can debate meaningfully about public policies and whether the outcomes of such debates will serve the community at large. Under Pericles, Thucydides shows us a city in which democracy had nothing to do with communal deliberation (at least explicitly), though the way of life and the regime were in name a democracy. If Pericles' citizens were to become the complete *erastes* of Athens, if they were to abstract themselves from their personal sufferings, if they were to become one, the city would function in its ideal perfection with debate as unnecessary as in Socrates' Callipolis. But, as the plague demonstrated, such perfection, such abstraction from body, such unity is impossible. There are bodies that divide, that offer different experiences, that present alternative visions that necessitate a democracy of many, not a monarchy of one.

It is in the Mytilenian Debate that we find proposals for alternate policies, and the arguments against and for the opportunity to express those alternate views. It is the demand for alternative views that wins and leads to the most humane policy, clothed in arguments of expediency. But such communal decision-making does not always provide the finer outcome, in particular when the arguments rely on accusations and incriminations, when they focus on personalities rather than policies, whether it be at Athens or in Syracuse. There is no assurance that the gift of Zeus will appear to speak in measured terms to the assembly; the more likely scenarios are what we find in Books 6 and 7 with the Sicilian campaign where the assembly, whether in Athens or Syracuse, tends to degenerate into the individual claims of individual leaders and where men like Nicias and Hermocrates become fearful of speaking. That is what happens to Nicias in the end. He has lost his earlier conviction that if he speaks openly his dissenting views, the Athenians might listen and show their capacity for change. This is the potential of democracy that Thucydides has shown us.

To describe Thucydides as hostile to democracy, as Hobbes did, to say that he least of all liked democracy, is too limiting, just as to describe Herodotus as an advocate of democracy ignores the complexity of his *Histories*. Thucydides recognizes democracy's potential in its openness to diverse opinions clashing against one another, opinions that arise because men—to borrow the language of today's discourse—are "embodied" in their individuality. To transform a city into a Periclean ideal ignores those bodies; to allow men to debate alternative policies acknowledges them. The challenge that Athenian democracy could not meet, however, was how to keep the private and the individual—from which differing opinions emerge, from which regimes gain the capacity to deal with an ever-changing world—from intruding into the debate and changing the focus from the welfare of the city to the welfare of the individual. Perhaps Thucydides is telling us, as will Rousseau in somewhat different language centuries later, that democracy is a regime that can only function insofar as we have gifts from Zeus. Pericles as the city's unifier was not such a gift. His vision could not incorporate bodies into one bodiless city. Diodotus, the son of Eucrates, who urged open debate with forward-looking policies that were not bound or limited by the past, was such a "gift of Zeus."

CHAPTER 4

Plato

and the Problematic Gentleness of Democracy

I

Plato, we know well, was no friend of democracy. It was, after all, the democratic regime that executed his hero, Socrates. Virtually every standard text on the history of political philosophy reminds us of this fact and of Plato's distaste for the demos. One can go from the rather blatant claims by Neal and Ellen Wood that "The Platonic teaching can be illuminated by placing it in its proper context as the product of an aristocratic mentality, distressed at the increasing 'vulgarization' of Athens" (1978, 126), or from G. E. M. de Ste. Croix (never one to mince words), who writes of "Plato, an arch-enemy of democracy" and comments that "Plato, one of the most determined and dangerous enemies that freedom has ever had, sneers at democracy" (1981, 412, 284), to the considerably more moderate Cynthia Farrar, who condemns Plato as antidemocratic because of his lack of concern with instilling competence and independence. She sees a Plato who believes that "Autonomy is not . . . possible for the vast majority of individuals, and it is not necessary" (1988, 268).

To show this hostility, all that these and other authors have to do is refer to the passages in Book 6 of the *Republic* where a large number of parables suggest the inadequacy of a democratic regime. To begin with, there is the parable of the boat, in which we see the demos portrayed as the owner of the boat; he is taller and stronger than the crew but somewhat deaf, with narrow vision, and generally not too knowledgeable about steering. Surrounded by a crew eager to take control, a crew fighting among themselves about who should rule (though each is incapable of justifying that rule), the owner is overcome as the crew subdue him with drink and spend his wealth (488a–e). Thus, Socrates would seem to suggest, democracy is ravaged by its crafty politicians because the dumb, nearsighted demos cannot defend itself against shrewd, self-interested men eager only for control over the resources of the ship and not concerned about its welfare. Meanwhile the man who is capable of rule, the stargazer who knows how to navigate to the desired locations, stands at the rear of the ship, unable and unwilling to join the competition for political control. In this parable of democracy, the stargazer's wisdom, which should make him the true leader of the ship, goes unacknowledged and untapped.

Or there is the parable of the demos as a wild beast whose passions and desires, moods and feelings, must be learned by the man who wishes to control it. Completely yielding to the beast, the man, knowing nothing about the truth concerning those desires and feelings—whether they are good or bad, shameful or noble—simply follows the desires of the beast and calls good what pleases it and shameful what annoys it. Neither the many nor those appealing to the many know the good or the noble, and thus they make no effort to bring the good into the political life of the city. They allow the city to sway with the passions of the beast, just so long as they can have power within the city.

Socrates creates yet another powerful image of the problems of democracy when he describes how the demos educates those young men who may indeed start off capable of accomplishing much good.

Whenever a great crowd is seated together in the *ecclēsia* or in the court or in the theater or military camp or any other common multitude called all together, with a great deal of uproar they blame some things and praise others, exaggerating each one, calling out and clapping. In addition, the rocks and the place in which they are gathered echo and make the noise of praise and blame two-fold. In such a situation, what sort of inclination will grab the young man? (492b–c)

Thus, the youth with potential are perverted by the political institutions of the democracy.

Such parables and such stories seem to leave no doubt about Socrates' hostility to democracy, to its dependence on the unfounded and uncertain whims of an unschooled mass of men who are manipulated by those skillful in appealing to their likes and dislikes, by those who know how to control their variable and uncertain opinions, rather than turning to those who have access to an unchanging truth. In these parables from the *Republic* Socrates makes clear the conflict between democracy and philosophy: the demos appears stupid, it cannot tell the difference between truth and mere opinion, it is governed by beastly passions, and it is ignorant of all sorts of important matters. Bad leaders emerge because the people who choose them have bad judgment, because they lack the philosophy that is needed to bring an end to the troubles of the life of men in cities.

To see this hostility to the democratic regime, however, as hostility towards and disdain for the individuals who make up the demos is to have a view of Socrates that is profoundly inconsistent with the Socrates of other dialogues, a Socrates who is committed to the possibilities of educating the individual, to talking to all who will listen, be they citizens or foreigners, old or young, male or female (e.g., *Apology* 23b). To take the parables of Book 6 as simply critical and dismissive of the majority of men is to fail to set those parables in the much larger context of the long dialogue that precedes and follows, of Socrates as an individual, and of Platonic thought in general. In this chapter I want to question the too-easy assumptions of Plato's negative attitude towards democracy and therefore the too-ready dismissal of his writings on democracy. This is not in any way to say that we must read Plato as an advocate of democratic regimes; certainly, he is not. But it is to suggest that Plato can help us reflect on democracy precisely because he takes seriously the assumptions underlying democratic regimes and points to issues that make democracy an interesting regime, not simply because it defines where power is located in ancient Athens but because democracies provide the bases for what Socrates cares most about: the activity of philosophy and the education of the young. Rather than being defensive and seeing Plato as opposed to democracy because of "aristocratic disdain" or "denial of autonomy" or claims to knowledge inaccessible to the many, I want to explore why democracy is of interest to Socrates, what issues it raises for him, and how these help us to understand the relation between philosophy and politics.

In Book 8 of the *Republic* Socrates gives a fictionalized account of the emergence of democracy as he traces the deterioration of regimes from the best down to the worst—from the rule of the philosopher down to the rule of the tyrant. Second to last in this sequence of deterioration, just prior to tyranny, is democracy. And in describing life in that city, Socrates asks: "Is not the gentleness of those who have been judged in the courts refined [*kompsē*]? Or have you never seen in such a city men who have been condemned to death or exile, no less remaining and wandering about in its midst, so that as a hero he wanders about while no one sees or pays any attention?" (558a). The condemned man remains a member of the democracy. One is, of course, reminded by this passage of the narrator of the entire *Republic* who has been condemned to die, indeed even was executed, and yet still very much wanders around the city in the cloak of the Platonic dialogues, performing much the same deeds he performed while alive and for which he was condemned to die. Does the gentleness of democracy towards the condemned allow the philosopher to rule as he never could even in a regime governed explicitly by the philosopher kings and queens identified in the fifth book of the *Republic*?[1] It is especially in the dramatic background to the dialogues that we can see how Socrates is a creature of democracy and no other regime. For all its dependence on false opinion, for all its foibles and difficulties, Plato through the dialogue acknowledges the centrality of democracy for the pursuit of philosophy.[2] In what follows, I look to the dramatic settings first,[3] and then reflect further on how the democracy of the *Republic* helps us understand some of the complex issues any democracy must address. Thus, I try to rise above ideological attacks against Plato and attend to what Plato via Socrates suggests we need to consider in constituting democratic regimes.[4]

II

The *Symposium* is Plato's dialogue on love. It is a series of nested speeches in which we learn of an evening when drinking is replaced by discourse meant to be in praise of love—of a passion that is unharnessed, a passion that perhaps captures the freedom central to the democratic regime.[5] Love is a god and therefore good, worthy of eulogy, and so each speaker competitively offers his own version of that praise.

Aristodemus, a young and ugly follower of Socrates, narrates the entire dialogue to Apollodorus, from whom we hear the report of the evening's speeches and events. As Aristodemus tells the story, the famous evening begins when he encounters a Socrates who has just finished bathing and who, contrary to his customary manner of going barefooted, has put on fine slippers. Socrates is on his way to the celebration at the home of Agathon, who has won the prize for the best tragedy at the Dionysian festival. Socrates (illustrating the distaste for the many that has fueled the claims of an antidemocratic Socrates) explains that he had fled yesterday's victory party at Agathon's house, fearing the mob (*ochlos*) that would gather there to celebrate Agathon's victory. But tonight, he continues, would be different. The *ochlos* would not be there. Insofar as we identify democracy with "the mob" and the regime described in Book 6 of the *Republic*, Socrates in this dialogue shows all the condescension for which many have condemned him, but insofar as we think of democracy as a series of institutional arrangements dependent on principles of freedom and openness and equality, we can see it as *the* regime that allows for its "citizens" to engage in philosophy and explore the good of the whole. The mob does not appear until the end of the dialogue, at which point openness and especially the freedom treasured earlier no longer define the relations among the participants in the evening's affairs. Instead, the mob brings with it tyranny, not democracy.

Socrates invites his friend Aristodemus—our narrator once removed—to join him at the dinner in Agathon's house on this second night of celebration. Aristodemus hesitates; he describes himself as a worthless man (*phaulos*, 174c), going unbidden to dine at the home of a wise man. He worries that Socrates will need to make an *apologia* for bringing such a common man to dine. As it turns out, no *apologia* is needed for this *phaulos* to become part of the community that meets at Agathon's house. While Socrates remains on a nearby porch in a trance, Aristodemus proceeds to Agathon's house where he finds the door wide open and an unqualified welcome from the host. No distinction is made between the small, ugly Aristodemus and the beautiful, "wise" Agathon— and from the warmth of the invitation to enter, there is no sense that this is a "worthless man" entering where he will not be equal to the others. Though we do not receive a report of his speech, they are all to participate together in the evening's events.

We see in Aristodemus' entrance to the party a variety of issues that confront all communities, but especially democracies:

who is included and who is excluded. If we talk about the democratic principle, as Socrates does in Book 8 of the *Republic*, as an equality that does not discriminate, or as Otanes did or Theseus in Euripides' play did when they placed power *en meson* ("in the middle"), then how are we to decide who is within the community and who is outside, who is in the middle and who is not, who is welcome to the dinner and who is to be excluded, who is worthless (*phaulos*) and who is wise, who is animal and who is human? In the way in which democratic principles function at Agathon's house, at least in the early part of the dialogue, all are welcomed. Distinctions between worthless and wise, superior and inferior, do not determine exclusion or inclusion. The political regime at Athens, though, must exclude. As Manville (1990, chap. 7) points out, this was the profound challenge for the new democracy at the end of the sixth century, namely, how to clarify who was a citizen and who was not. It was difficult, because the equality principle used to break down the old aristocratic principle of family was incapable of articulating precisely how to set those new boundaries. Insofar as Athens must explore its membership laws, it dismisses the democratic principles Socrates identifies in Book 8, and indeed reminds us of the problems we currently face at all our borders about who can be welcomed and who cannot, as we are forced to discriminate against the fundamental principles of democratic equality.

Once Aristodemus joins the dinner party, we find an easiness and freedom, a certain lackadaisical quality characterizing the relationships between the host and guests and others. Agathon tries to play the master by ordering his servants to bring Socrates from the neighbor's porch to the dinner, but Aristodemus restrains him from forcing Socrates. "Let him be [*eate*]," he repeats twice (175b). There is to be no compulsion. Socrates will come when it pleases Socrates, not when it pleases Agathon. Freedom is to characterize the evening. Socrates is not compelled to attend the dinner (or to rule). Likewise, a lack of compulsion pervades the dinner. The servants are released to prepare whatever meal they wish and the flute girl is left alone, not forced to entertain but allowed to be with the women within, "if she wishes" (176e). Compulsion disappears from the dramatic setting, as the evening's symposiasts prepare to discuss the freest of passions in a setting that comes to resemble the assembly.

In Book 8 of the *Republic* the regime of complete equality and consequent freedom deteriorates rapidly into the least free and least equal regime, namely, a tyranny. But that does not happen at Agathon's house—at least at first. Instead, there is a gentlemanly order preserved through respect for the particular form of knowledge that each participant brings to the dinner setting. Xenophon in his *Reminiscences of Socrates* has his Socrates repeat the parable of the boat that I cited earlier from the *Republic*, only in Xenophon's version the men on board the ship obey the stargazer because it is in their interest to obey one who knows. How could anyone refuse to be obedient to or be persuaded by (the Greek unites these words in one) someone who is an expert? The refusal to take the advice of the expert is punishment in itself. In such a setting democracy is neither mob rule nor competition for power; it is the acceptance of the wisdom of men who know because it is in one's own self-interest to do so. This, we should note, is the one dialogue in which Socrates admits to being an expert, albeit on the topic of love. If we think beyond democracy as being simply the assembly and the translation of popular will into public policy, we see in the openness of the setting for the *Symposium*, the democratic qualities of the dialogue.

At Agathon's house the night before, when the *ochlos* was there, the guests, as they themselves put it, got a thorough soaking. They did not act in their own self-interest, as the hangovers the next day made clear, especially to Pausanias and Aristophanes (176a–b) In the restructured setting where Socrates has now arrived, the doctor among those assembled, Eryximachus by name, advises abstinence, and the assembly listens. He knows from his practice of medicine that drunkenness is harsh for men. No compulsion is needed to restrain drinking, only self-interested obedience to one who knows. Indeed, the assembled group concludes, through the voice of the doctor, "It has seemed best [using the language of the assembly—*dedoktai*] that each one drinks as much as each one wishes, that there be no compulsion" (176e). The unity between freedom and authority is achieved in Agathon's house through wisdom. Self-rule, the absence of compulsion, and equality, all meld in the dramatic setting of the dialogue, but only—an important *caveat*—if the *ochlos* is absent.

The evening described in the *Symposium* continues in this fashion, as the characters mimic the behavior of citizens in the *ecclēsia*. The assembled guests now debate what they are to do, since they have agreed not to compete in drinking. As a community they need to define that communal action which will engage them during the evening ahead. The doctor proposes to honor the god of love with speeches. Socrates with an unaccustomed note of self-assurance asserts in the language of the assembly: "No one will vote against you" and, using another term common from the discourse of the assembly, he sets the group off on their series of speeches "with good luck" (177d–e). Since I am focusing on the dramatic setting here and not on the content of the marvelous speeches for which the *Symposium* is renowned, I will only note that apart from the disorderly hiccoughs of the comic poet Aristophanes (who disrupts the Athenian democracy as well with his outrageous parodies of the Athenian political system), the evening proceeds in an orderly fashion, each participant speaking in turn, drawing on his particular excellence to praise love (and, incidentally, to praise himself as well). The communal activity communally and freely decided upon has the good fortune that Socrates had wished for it.

Nevertheless, sometime during the speeches and the moderate drinking the community at Agathon's house has transformed itself. The door is closed, the order created by the community once established must confine membership to those who have agreed to conduct themselves according to those principles. When the group in the *Symposium* hears knocking at the door, Agathon (reverting to giving orders rather than allowing each to do as he or she wishes) tells his servants: "If it is some one of our companions, invite him in. If not, say that we are not drinking but now going to bed" (212d). Now there are friends and there are those who are not friends. The open door that so welcomed Aristodemus at the beginning of the dialogue has been shut.[6] The longer they have praised love and functioned within their own community, the further they have moved from the openness and democratic decision processes that defined the early evening.

The new visitor to Agathon's house, though, is not restrained by closed doors or excuses. It is Alcibiades, the enfant terrible of Athenian politics, he who has many lovers, wins many Olympic medals, bears the emblem of Eros on his shield, divorces his wife after physically carrying her to court—and more. He is outrageously flamboyant, attractive, and yet repulsive in his self-promotion. He has upset the life of Athenian democracy profoundly,[7] and he is about to upset the order of the community in Agathon's house. Once he enters, all the current members cry out loudly and ask him to join them; he *is* attractive. With Alcibiades and the disruption he brings with him, commands and compulsion fully replace the choice and freedom that had been there during the earlier part of the evening. The servants no longer do as they wish; Agathon now commands them—to take off Alcibiades' sandals, to pour drinks for everyone. They no longer are the judges of what needs to be done. They listen to a master, not themselves. Fear and threats appear, albeit all in good humor.

Alcibiades, upon discovering that Socrates is present, pleads for protection from his violence and then pronounces on his own, against the previous communally accepted and voted upon decisions. Eryximachus reminds him it was resolved (*edoxe*, 214b), but the resolutions of the community at Agathon's house mean little to Alcibiades and he asserts that there shall be drinking and that he himself shall be in charge of the subsequent communal drinking. Alcibiades swoops down on this community, charms the assembled members in Agathon's house, just as he charmed those who sat in the assembly on the Pnyx, and wins their support, turning them into a "mob." He becomes their tyrant and with little more than a sweet and entrancing speech suddenly all previous order, all attention to the wisdom of the specialist, all equality of speech disappear before the elegant and handsome young man. In vain, the doctor Eryximachus who had given the original advice about moderation in drink tries to reinstate the original regime, recalling the order and nature of the speeches to which they had originally agreed. It is the tyrant who creates the mob in this story, not the mob who creates the tyrant.

Alcibiades unilaterally, without approval from all, indeed rejecting the commonly agreed-upon decision, selects his own subject. He happens to decide to speak on Socrates, and as a result we fortunately get one of the greatest speeches to be found about this strange man. But in presenting this speech, Alcibiades rejects the democratic decision-making processes by which a proposal was voted and acted upon by the participants. As in Athens, he plays the tyrant. Once Alcibiades finishes his speech, a mass of celebrants comes through the gates and, as Aristodemus reports, "everything was full of confusion, and there was no longer any order [kosmōi], and they were forced [anagkazesthai] to drink a great deal of wine" (223b). Some of the original guests escape.[8] The rest (except, of course, Socrates) drink themselves into a mindless stupor.

The transformation of the party brought about by Alcibiades' entrance suggests the inadequate defenses of a regime such as that founded in the early evening in Agathon's house. At first, membership was open, decisions were made according to what seemed best to the whole community, no one was compelled to do that which he—or she—did not wish to do, advice in the interest of all was respected. But such a regime is unstable and subject to manipulation by an Alcibiades, a vibrant young man who wants attention, who is eager to be "first," and who is not motivated by principles of obedience to those who know because he assumes that he alone has knowledge, or at least whatever knowledge is relevant to the issue at hand. He desires power over others; he commands and, most important, he allures. Even those who have enjoyed the quiet evening are all abuzz when Alcibiades enters. The regime at Agathon's house is susceptible to such a transformation. The men who founded the orderly regime at Agathon's become the mob themselves in the presence of an Alcibiades.

For an individual like Socrates, Alcibiades' arrival makes no difference. He leaves to carry on the day as usual before retiring at home. The disruptive influence of an Alcibiades does not affect the life of such a person. But for the others, either they must depart quickly from Agathon's home or be drugged by the wine into slumber. Alcibiades is the winner among those vying to control the dumb and slightly deaf shipowner—whether the shipowner be the citizens of Athens gathered in the assembly or the select few gathered in the home of the winning playwright. Socrates alone survives the transformation of the dramatic setting from one of order to disorder, from a regime that believes in the democratic principles of self-government and openness to the tyranny of Alcibiades. The dramatic dialogue shows us a Socrates impervious to the political organization of a community. Democracy succeeding or failing in this context has no impact on him. He proceeds with his day as usual.

As we know only too well, this is not the case outside the dialogue, where Socrates could not so easily ignore the democratic regime that would ultimately execute him. But the democracy of Plato's dialogues allows those whom the Athenian democracy condemned—even those whom they executed—to continue to roam freely and to speak to us.

In Book 1 of the *Republic* we find ourselves in the home of the metic (resident alien) Cephalus, an arms manufacturer. Socrates has come as a guest, but the evening soon turns into a competition, not of speeches as in the *Symposium*, but for control over the hearts and minds of the young men who are gathered in the private house of a metic and not in the open setting of the Pnyx where the mountains echo the praise and blame of the multitudes. Socrates competes first with the old man Cephalus, who quickly yields when Socrates asks some difficult questions about the implementation of Cephalus' definition of justice. Age is no claim to authority. Socrates competes with poets who are cited by the young Polemarchus, but the poets are no help. While they can tell us that justice is helping your friends and harming your enemies, they give little guidance about who is a friend and who is an enemy. Finally, Socrates competes with the Sophist Thrasymachus, who knows precisely how to implement his definition of justice as the interest of the stronger, but who falters when he must face the issue of who is stronger and what is in one's interest. Age, poets, realpolitik all fall in Book 1, so we are left with the question of what principle of political order one is to follow in the wake of those littering Book 1.

In Book 5 of the *Republic* we learn the answer—sort of. Book 5 is a new beginning. In many ways, with a host of allusions, it recalls the very beginning of the *Republic* and the physical setting of the dialogue in the Piraeus, the center of democratic resistance among the Athenians (Bloom 1968, 440n. 3). The dramatic interaction among the characters achieves this recollection of place, just before Socrates proposes the most radical details of his Callipolis, the city in which the guardians and warriors are to have no private property or families, where women are to be educated along with the men, and where philosophers are to be the kings or queens. The dramatic setting which is a preface to the establishment of the city of philosopher-rulers, warriors, and artisans in neat hierarchical order depends on the procedures of the democratic regime at Athens. Polemarchus and Adeimantus, using the language of the Athenian judicial system, stop the flow of the conversation to say that they will not release Socrates; instead, they bring a "charge" against him for "stealing" a part of the argument. He must discuss the casual reference he made in the previous book to the community of wives and children among the rulers in the city that they are founding together. Adeimantus informs Socrates in language common to the law courts and the assembly: "It has seemed best to us . . . not to release you until you go through this part of the argument" (449e–50a). Glaucon casts a vote (*psēphos*) supporting his brother, and Thrasymachus, using the language of the democratic assembly, announces: "It has seemed best to us" (450a). Thrasymachus continues to speak as if he were in a law court using the language of involuntary manslaughter and the purification for murder. The institutional setting of Athens here prepares the way for Socrates' investigation of the city according to one's dreams and prayers. Must one live in a democracy to dream of a Callipolis?

While the most outstanding elements of Callipolis for us (and most likely for the Greeks as well) are the three waves (first, of sexual equality; then, of communism; and finally, of philosopher-rulers), we find embedded in those proposals recollections of the democratic institutions of Athens, albeit altered, but nevertheless providing guidance as Socrates explores the regime of our dreams. If we look at Callipolis with a bit of a sideways glance at Athens, we almost see a reformed Athens. As he founded his famous city in speech in the previous books, Socrates had ignored the institutions which allowed the cities of Greece to function; there are no courts in Callipolis, no assemblies, no involuntary manslaughter. While the assembly never makes an appearance in Callipolis and, with the communism of property and wives,

Socrates suggests that law courts will never be necessary, we find other aspects of Athens' political machinery employed by the inhabitants of Callipolis. In writing about ancient democracy, M. I. Finley had described its linchpins as the lot and remuneration—the lot to assign political offices, and remuneration for participation in the assembly (1973, 19). Whereas lot in Athens determines who takes on various administrative responsibilities, in Socrates' Callipolis the (admittedly somewhat manipulated) lot assigns men and women to one another for the purposes of mating. Marriages, not offices, depend on the fall of the lot machine (460a). The political machinery of Athenian democracy intrudes here into what had been the most private of relations, emphasizing the full "publicization" of all things in this regime.[9] Likewise, remuneration for participation is here as well: the guardians and warriors, with no private property, are completely supported by the city, being paid far more than the one or two obols a day an Athenian citizen received to attend the assembly.[10] Underlying both systems is the expectation that the work for the common welfare of the community requires compensation; neither philosophers nor Athenian citizens willingly engage in political life out of unfettered altruism.

Socrates does not give power to the many in Callipolis, his beautiful city, nor does he wish to offer an equality of participation in the structure of the city or to build on a tradition of communal decision-making such as characterizes the venue for philosophic discourse. With the three classes performing their separate roles, there is certainly no *isonomia*, no equality before and within the law, and certainly since some, the philosophers, know the truth, there is no need to bring men together to deliberate on the best course of action—as there is among the interlocutors of a Platonic dialogue. Though we do find that the democratic institutions of Athens offer principles that can be incorporated into the city of our dreams, Callipolis is not a democracy. Socrates calls it an aristocracy, the rule of the best. But the *Republic*, like the

Symposium, shows how the discourse among the Platonic characters relies on democratic principles of engagement, equality, and communal decision-making. Philosophy as an activity in which Platonic characters engage (as opposed to the state of ruling) has much more in common with democracy than it does with aristocracy.

Nevertheless, Socrates also points to some of the problems that democratic principles might pose for a philosopher. In the first moments of the dialogue there is an interchange in which Polemarchus responds to Socrates' resistance to his request that Socrates remain in the Piraeus: "Do you see how many we are? . . . Be stronger [*kreitton*] than these or remain here" (327c). Socrates inquires whether he might not persuade these greater numbers and Polemarchus responds that persuasion will not work if they choose not to listen. Force in terms of numbers dominates in this scene; as in a democracy, numbers, not reason or knowledge, matter.[11] By the time we are well into the dialogue in Book 5, we still find the power of numbers apparently dominating the direction of the conversation. The mocking tone remains, the orderly sense of how the group proceeds pervades the scene, but the recollections of the first scene remind us that Polemarchus' threat of the force of numbers stands behind the democratic assembly's (or the community's at Cephalus' house) decision process.

The challenge that Socrates poses for Thrasymachus when Thrasymachus defines justice as the interest of the stronger (*kreittonos*, 338c) is how we may know who is stronger. This is not a challenge to democratic assemblies. The answer concerning the stronger is obvious; it is the majority. This is true for the dramatic characters in the dialogue where the conversation proceeds by democratic vote. Socrates, constrained by the vote of the majority to discuss what he says he would prefer not to, concludes his proposals for the city of his dreams with the presentation of communism of property, equality among the men and women in the activities of war, and rule by philosopher-rulers—all, but mostly the last, suggestions worthy of the greatest ridicule by those assembled (473e–74a). So the democracy of Cephalus' house compels Socrates to explain himself, to offer his *apologia*, as the democracy of Athens did too. In Athens, the majority, the greater number, the "stronger," were not satisfied with the *apologia*. It is unclear whether the characters of the *Republic* accept Socrates' speech. At first, certainly, they do not, and in Book 6, particularly, Socrates must continue his *apologia* (488a, 490a) before the unconvinced judges at Cephalus' house.

IV

In the very first scene of the *Republic*, again in the discussion with Thrasymachus in Book 1, and at the beginning of Book 5, democracy appears as a regime where numbers compel and force dominates. A very different perspective on democracy emerges when Socrates offers his description of it as a regime in the speech of the dialogue. In Book 8 Socrates gives an account of democracy which seems to have little relation to the regime in operation in Athens or in the community at Cephalus' house, where the language of democracy serves as the directive force for the dramatic characters. Second to last in the sequence of the deterioration of regimes, just prior to tyranny, is democracy. Most characteristic of life in that city is the gentleness we noticed before, especially to those condemned in the courts to death who nevertheless continue to wander about the city's streets with no one seeing or paying any attention (558a). Shortly after commenting on the freedom of the condemned man in a democracy, Socrates says: "The greatest point of liberty . . . of the many, however much it comes to be in such a city [democracy] is when the slaves, male and female, are not less free than those who bought them. And among the women towards the men and among the men towards the women how much equality is there before the law [*isonomia*] and freedom, I almost forgot to say" (563b). It gets even more extreme than equality between women and men; animals are freer in a democracy than anywhere else and horses and asses are accustomed to journeying freely and haughtily, bumping into whomever they encounter on the road if he does not stand aside (563c).

These passages about the gentleness of democracy (in contrast to the force implicit in the principle of majority rule) give us some sense of the theoretical challenge Socrates finds in democracies. Democracy is a regime that does not discriminate, or as Adeimantus in the same section notes, quoting Aeschylus: "We say whatever comes to our lips" (563c). We do not find in a democracy a clear articulation of the differences between the master and the slave, between the male and the female, between those condemned to die and those who are to live freely, between blasphemy and speech which is not blasphemous. This is quite different from the analysis of Book 6, where the images that evoke the democratic regime of Athens suggest the inadequacies of democracy because it appeals to its citizens' passions and depends on their unjustified opinions (and where Socrates does indeed seem to be scorning the masses as stupid and uninformed).

One of the curiosities of the democratic regime described in Book 8 of the *Republic* is that it seems to bear so little resemblance to the democracy of Athens as we know it from historical and literary sources—even less resemblance than Callipolis, where at least the use of the lot reminds us of the lot in Athens and where the participants receive remuneration. In Book 8 there is no discussion of the institutions of democracy, but there is discussion of what we today would call the cultural and emotional life of democratic citizens. Socrates here identifies as distinctive about democracy, not the force implicit in the focus on numbers, but the extreme apathy that goes along with the extreme of freedom and the extreme of equality. No one seems to care what others do or think; that's why the condemned man still roams the street; that's why animals do not get out of the way of human beings. Everyone—in our modern liberal lingo—does his, her, its own thing. There is no shared decision-making process, no meetings of the assembly; if the courts do function to condemn someone, their decisions matter little. *Parrhēsia* (freedom of speech) is indeed present, as in Athens, but at Athens it had political connotations, the freedom to speak in the assembly where citizens debate various public policies. In the democracy of Book 8, it is open for any one to say anything anywhere or to do anything anywhere, precisely because no one cares.

This excessive freedom, this apathy of the democracy of Book 8, means that no one has to rule in this regime, no common decisions are made, no wars are to be fought. No Socrates would be forced by Polemarchus to accompany him home and become the leader of the little community founded in his father's house. No philosophers would be dragged down from their contemplation of the sun to rule in the darkness of the cave. No women would be forced to give up their children for strangers to nurse. This is a regime of complete privacy—or to use the Greek term, complete idiocy. Unlike the democracy that Pericles had described in his Funeral Oration, where the citizen uninvolved in the political life of the city was considered useless, it is a regime of complete tolerance where no one judges one person useless and another useful. It is a regime perhaps best captured by the Theseus of Euripides' *Suppliant Women* (which was in part a paean to the newly founded democracy). He had spoken in praise of Athens' equality, where he who wishes to shine forth speaks and he who does not so wish keeps silent, "What greater equality could there be in the city?" he asks (441). Insofar as critics today bewail the lack of involvement, the apathy of the contemporary democratic citizen, we must keep in mind as well whether certain democratic principles may work against such expectations. The tolerant democracy of Book 8 can be so tolerant because of the apathy of all its inhabitants—citizens, slaves, animals.

While the aristocracy, as Socrates calls it, of Callipolis is created out of the words of Socrates and his companions as they search for the just individual, the democracy of Book 8 arises in Socrates' story from a revolution, from the desire for new things. In language that foreshadows the Aristotelian discussion of revolutions, Socrates presents the transformation from oligarchy to democracy as a debate about the foundations of the claims to rule. The rich oligarchs, caring only about the acquisition of wealth and not paying attention to the education of the poor, letting the poor "take pleasure in whatever they might wish" (557b), leave open the possibility for the poor to ask why the wealthy, who are few and weak, should rule when they, the poor, are strong. The wealthy had not "educated" the poor to understand the foundation of rule on the claim to the control of resources rather than on the strength of numbers. They did not teach the poor to look to criteria that justify rule by the few rather than the many. Unlike the transformations of other regimes that Socrates describes, of aristocracy to timocracy, of timocracy to oligarchy, which occur because of the private desire for wealth or prestige, the transformation of oligarchy to democracy is based on the claim to rule as a principle of justice, the principle that the strong— here defined as those whose bodies are strong—ought to rule.

Socrates describes the events that would lead up to this revolution; he says:

Whenever the rulers and the ruled approach one another either on a journey on the road or in some other common activity, or on an embassy or an expedition or sailing together or being in the army together or seeing each other, the poor are in no way scorned by the rich, but often the poor man, suntanned and lean, stands next to the rich man, pale and fat, and sees him without breath and at a loss. Do you not think that he would think that such men are rich through his own cowardice and that each one would say to another whenever they are together in private, "The men are ours. They are worth nothing" (556c–d).

The poor who are strong in body question the rule of the rich who are weak in body, and so democracy here begins with the rule of the strong against the weak, the strong defined simply in terms of physical power of the individual citizens. For democracy this dependence on the physical strength of the individual gets carried over to strength defined in terms of numbers as well. "I think," says Socrates, "democracy comes into being whenever the victorious poor kill some, exile others, and hand over to the rest an equal share of the regime and of the offices and for the most part the offices are distributed by lot in it" (557a).

This is a curious, abstract definition of democracy. While certainly in Athens offices were distributed by lot, and despite Finley's claim that this is one of the linchpins of ancient democracy, as well it might be, nevertheless ancient Athenian democracy entailed much more than distribution by lot. Historians of ancient democracy today debate with great energy whether the assembly or the law courts had the true political power in the city. Neither of these institutions at the core of the Athenian political experience enters Socrates' definition of democracy. The language of the law courts and the assembly where citizens must decide "what appears best" is left for the dramatic setting that introduces Book 5. With the condemned man walking casually along the streets of the city of this democracy in Book 8, the law courts seem to have no role, making no difference in the lives of citizens. This is, as Socrates presents it, a democracy without institutions. His understanding of the political world is a way of life, an attitude, and particularly an epistemological stance. It is not a mechanism for putting policies into practice or bringing together viewpoints to create policies.

Thus, what is curious about Socrates' discussion of democracy is its very apolitical nature. The freedom (*eleutheria*) that fills this discourse about democracy gives us a politeia—a regime — without politics. There are no choices, no leaders, no executions, no compulsion, and especially no conflict. And, as if to remind us of his story about the philosophers who have seen the sun outside the cave and are forced back down to rule in the best city, and of his own situation at the beginning of the dialogue when he is forced to stay in the Piraeus by the young men who wish to hear him talk, with all this in the readers' minds, Socrates adds: "In this city there is no compulsion to rule, not even if one is capable of rule, nor again to be ruled, if one does not wish to be, nor when others are at war, to be at war" (557e). Democracy is an individualized, privatized, idiotic regime that shows how the institutions of Athenian democracy—forcing citizens to rule through the lot and to reach judgments in the law courts and the numerous assemblies—seem to work in opposition to principles that underlie the regime he calls a democracy here.

As an Athenian citizen, one was subject to the lot, by which one was placed in political office, by which one could be forced to rule. Aristophanes writes a comedy, the *Acharnians*, about a man who wishes to be at peace with Sparta when the rest of his city is at war with Sparta. This is a comic proposal for the Athenians, intended to make them laugh while they saw the allure of peace, but Socrates introduces the private treaty-maker into his description of the paradigmatic democracy. Dikaiopolis, the (anti-) hero of Aristophanes' *Acharnians*, is not, according to Socrates, an anomaly but the embodiment of the democratic character. Even Socrates, the most private of men who scorned political office and preferred one-on-one conversations to speeches before the many, is forced in Athens to go to war. From Alcibiades we hear about his battlefield performance at Delium, and from Socrates himself, during his speech before the jury that is trying him on charges of introducing new gods into the city and corrupting the young, we learn that he served on the *boulē*, the administrative council of the assembly (*Apology* 32b). And, of course, the mere fact that he was brought to trial shows his involvement with the institutions of the city of Athens. Or, in the dramatic context of the dialogue which recaptures the democratic institutions of Athens, we find the compulsion to participate—on Socrates as well as on, for example, Thrasymachus in Book 1, who is forced to stay at Cephalus' house and continue the debate. If only in mocking fashion, Socrates is caught up in the setting of the courts by Thrasymachus in Book 1 and by the assembly of young men in Book 5. This democratic regime of the dialogic setting with all the allusions to the democratic institutions of Athens hardly allows each member to do whatever he wants. There is this strangeness, then, that the explicit description of democracy in Book 8 has so little to do with the political life of Athens or the dialogic setting that draws on that life.

The democracy of Book 8 is what we today might call a tolerant society. Socrates describes it as being multihued—attractive to women and young boys—with its multitude of types. Doing whatever one wishes, being unrestrained by the judgments of others, allows for political apathy and with that apathy comes a withdrawal from judgment. The democracy of Book 8 is tolerant precisely because no one cares whether one's neighbors are good or bad, foreigners or slaves. No one is prepared to make judgments. To make such judgments one must be involved, one must care whether the citizens are good or bad, where the regime draws its boundaries between insider and outsider, where it makes its distinctions between master and slave. What freedom exists in this regime is based on indifference; likewise, for equality. There is no conscious statement of a principle such as all men are created equal, or even all Athenian men over the age of eighteen are created equal. Rather, it is based on the refusal to be sufficiently involved to decide how to distinguish between equal and unequal, between citizen and foreigner, where to draw the line between good and bad, between human and animal. The democracy that Plato has Socrates describe here is hardly the regime that executed Socrates for corrupting the young, for the democracy of the *Republic* would not recognize corruption; in fact, that is what allows this democracy to deteriorate into the most corrupt regime of tyranny. But before we get to the tyrannical regime, we should realize that it is in a democracy of the Athenian sort where the inhabitants cannot be apathetic, where the decisions and choices must be made, where principles of policy must be articulated, that Socrates will be executed. There will be judgments of what is good and what is bad, though those judgments may be faulty. In the democracy of Book 8 there will simply be no judgment.

The curiosity about this democracy remains how little it has in common with the city of Athens—though we must notice, as well, some similarities with the aristocracy of Callipolis. It is in the democracy of Book 8 that we can imagine the community and equality of the sexes described as part of Callipolis. Leo Strauss, in his analysis of Socrates' Callipolis in his essay on Plato in *The City and Man*, argues for the impossibility of the just city (i.e., Callipolis) and makes the following claims:

> The just city is against nature because the equality of the sexes and absolute communism are against nature. It holds no attraction for anyone except for such lovers of justice as are willing to destroy the family as something essentially conventional and to exchange it for a society in which no one knows of parents, children, and brothers and sisters who are not conventional. ([1964] 1978, 127)

But in the democracy of Book 8 where everything is open, where everyone does whatever he or she wishes, there are no limits and there can be no distinction between what is by nature and what is by convention; there are no distinctions made between the male and the female, and there can be no family since that again suggests boundaries, which are not part of the apathetic, tolerant regime that has been given the name of democracy. The city that Strauss claims is opposed to nature is not only Callipolis with its equality of the sexes and its absolute communism, but also the so-called democracy of Book 8 that would allow for the conditions necessary for certain aspects of Callipolis to be instituted.

When we look at the democracy of Plato's *Republic*, considerable confusion sets in, since this democracy has elements that unite it with the city of Callipolis but virtually none of the elements of the democratic regime of Athens. We can ask, for instance, where is the fluctuation of Thucydides' democracy, where is the participatory ideal of Pericles' Funeral Oration, the ideal that has been so attractive to the mythmakers of the twentieth century. And where are the institutions that we all now associate with one regime or another? In particular, where are the assemblies and the juries? All those institutions entail an active citizenry, however much historians today may debate the numbers actually involved in those activities. For those citizens active in the life of the city, there must be some discrimination, some conception of the best, on the basis of which they are able to act. In the private subjective freedom of the democracy of Book 8, there is neither the best nor a claim to have discovered it. Instead there is delight in the multicolored cloak of all colors, not just "good" colors. Thus, there can be no fluctuations as citizens debate the good and the bad, as they are swayed from one position to another, since they hold no position. Thus, there can be no participation as there is no commitment, and no communal action, since no one can define the community.

In Book 9 of the *Republic*, Socrates shows us how this failure to discriminate deteriorates rapidly into tyranny. Tyranny carries the failure to discriminate even further, for it is a regime in which the ruler does not see any difference between himself and the gods, between his mother and all other women, between his subjects and his slaves. The tyrant perceives no limits on his actions or his desires, and while tyranny, like democracy, is apolitical in its abstraction from choice, it introduces a violence that is absent from the gentle, apathetic democracy of toleration of Book 8.

V

Behind all of my discussion here, of course, is the caveat that we should not read Plato as pro- or anti-democracy. In the past, readings of this kind by authors such as Karl Popper or more recently by Neal and Ellen Wood have done much to dismiss Plato as worse than irrelevant in a world that treasures equality and the opportunity for a multiplicity of life styles. He has been portrayed as dangerous and, with his insistence on the possibility of Truth, as a precursor of totalitarianism. To so dismiss him (admittedly less common now than right after the Second World War) is to ignore the impact that the democratic institutions (in which he, his friends, and his family functioned) had on his conceptualization of the human and the political problem. His analyses of human organization drew from the underlying assumptions of Athenian democracy—an equality, that must always be faced with the problem of boundaries, i.e., who is included in that democracy. By going beyond the plethora of institutions that marked Athenian democracy, Plato in both the *Symposium* and the *Republic* homed in on that underlying principle and its theoretical implications; not on the autonomy and the self-expression of the many, not on the will of the people, but on the acceptance of the principle of openness and thus a resistance to discrimination, whether it be between the ugly and the beautiful, the male and the female, the wise and the foolish.

While in the political realm such openness may lead to apathy and therewith to tolerance—and perhaps, as in the Socratic scenario of Book 9 of the *Republic*, to tyranny—philosophy requires, as the dramatic settings of the dialogues make very clear, that openness, that initial refusal to discriminate, that dismissal of false or thoughtlessly constructed boundaries. The democracy of Book 8 is similar to philosophy; it does not dismiss the slave (*Meno*) nor does it assume that man is not an animal (*Politicus*).

The problem for democracy—in profound contrast to philosophy—is that the very openness that characterizes its regime brings about its own destruction, for it remains incapable of discriminating against those who will undermine its openness—the tyrant, the demagogue like Alcibiades, and the physically strong. Underlying the practices of Athenian democracy, Plato discovers not what we in the modern world would want him to discover, the sovereignty of the people, the autonomy of the individual, and so forth, but the openness of equality and the apathy that may go along with it. While the philosopher thrives under these conditions of openness and equality which allow for the investigation of the multitude of possible ideas, from the obvious to the absurd (merely consider the content of the two dialogues I have discussed), the political world in contrast must have its limits, its points of discrimination, indeed its punishments and its execution of the man whom it finds guilty. The city must define its friends and its enemies as Polemarchus, following the poets, had suggested early in the dialogue; it must decide who can and who cannot participate in the debates in the assembly no matter how far the net is cast; it must decide whether one is eligible for office (the Athenian *dokimasia*), and once one has served in an office whether one has performed honestly (the *euthunē*); it must decide whether the decrees of the assembly accord with past traditions and so forth.

So while the principles of equality and openness are at the heart of the ancient democratic regime, they cannot be fully carried out lest the regime dissolve first into the apathetic democracy of Book 8 of the *Republic* and then into the tyranny of Book 9, lest it be incapable of performing the functions any regime must perform. The theoretical necessities of openness and equality and freedom of a democracy (which underlie the philosophic endeavor as well) can undermine, indeed must undermine the political principles of a democratic regime which is required to make choices, i.e., to distinguish. Plato's writing here uncovers the not surprising tensions between political practice and political principles. What Plato adds to this understanding is the critical, though certainly not negative, elaboration of what democracy at its roots entails, the contradictions that work to undermine it, and the openness that is at the beginning of the philosophic endeavor and is dependent on democratic principles.

For Socrates the danger of equality in the democratic regime is not that it elevates those who are of lesser worth—slaves, artisans, women—but that it allows us to sidestep the decisions that any political regime requires. It is here that philosophy enters, for philosophy is to lead us to the capacity to make those judgments, those decisions. The problem that remains, though, as we learn from the conversations between Socrates and Glaucon about philosophy and the forms to which the philosophers seek to gain access, is whether the knowledge to which philosophy aspires is ever accessible, whether the ascent from the cave into the full light of the sun is ever possible—and thus whether we may be left living in a world of indecision where democracy, insofar as it is gentle, is "the best regime." Plato's study of democracy is more than a study of which political regime we might choose if we were in the position of the seven Persian conspirators of Book 3 of Herodotus. It is to make us aware of some of the profound tensions at the heart of democratic theory and thus—as I read Plato—to move us beyond the political world of contradictions to the philosophical challenge of transcending those contradictions.

Aristotle:

Democracy and the Ambiguities of Nature

I

Jacob Klein in a paper simply entitled "The Political Thought of Plato and Aristotle" concludes his analysis of Plato's *Politicus* and Aristotle's *Politics* by adding what he calls "A short last remark." It is: "[T]he most significant difference between Aristotle and Plato is the total lack of playfulness in Aristotle's work" (1977, 21). This comment followed a paper in which Klein had produced a recitation of Aristotle's multiple typologies of regimes: the many forms of oligarchy, of democracy (those in which equality is more important, those in which there is a low property qualification, those in which all citizens of unquestioned descent participate, those in which the laws rule, those in which the citizens rule). There were as well many forms of kingship, from shared rule to absolute rule and all the stages in between. Typologies have never been my favorite sport and I have to admit an occasional weariness with Aristotle when he takes us into elaborate typological excursions. To have yet another recitation of these typologies did not make Klein's paper a particularly engaging one—until I reached that last line. That "short last remark" captured for me why Aristotle proceeds through his typologies as he does.

Aristotle is indeed not "playful" about politics; he clearly takes politics seriously. In part he expresses that seriousness by exploring the multiple alternative possibilities. This he does in contrast to Plato who, despite the fact that his teacher Socrates was executed by the city, takes a more playful view towards political life. For Plato the reform of political regimes seems far less likely and, with the move that we find at least in the *Republic* towards an internalization of virtue, the good human being can exist independently of the regime. When the crowd invades Agathon's house bringing drunkenness and chaos, Socrates remains unchanged. In many ways, he exists above the regime; he is not a product of it. As a result, the study of political life can have the playfulness that Klein suggested—a playfulness that moves us beyond the political world. For Aristotle it is through political life that most human beings achieve the capacity to become good, full human beings. Politics matters; the multiplicity of regimes matters. The alternative possibilities for political engagement, for the exercise of justice, for an accord with nature, all matter. What regime we live in has consequences directly for the lives we can lead. Whereas the *Republic* imagines the best city with regard to order and stability and the "welfare of the whole," Aristotle looks to the types of regimes that may allow the individual to reach a fulfillment not possible in other realms of human activity.

That Aristotle may not have Plato's playfulness, however, does not mean that Aristotle's writings are any more straightforward than Plato's. Since Aristotle does not write dialogues like Plato, there is too often the tendency to read Aristotle as if he were offering pronouncements on this or that. We quote Aristotle easily: "Man is a political animal"; "The citizen shares in offices and judgments"; "The male is superior to the female"; but we often fail to recognize the tentativeness of these so-easily quoted statements. Though Aristotle does not use the dialogue form of his own teacher, Plato, his work is, like Plato's, often aporetic, without a clear answer. A statement that appears as an assertion may be considered more like a challenge with a hidden question mark that turns the assertion into a field of exploration, to be questioned, to be tested by what we observe, by what we hear our companions say. The difficulty with much of the scholarship on Aristotle has often been the tendency to turn sentences posed as problems into Aristotelian dogma when in fact Aristotle's writings retain the aporetic quality of his teacher. To ignore the aporetic elements is to lose a sense of the subtlety of his analyses and the important qualifications that he raises about his own claims.

Important as well is the need to resist the temptation to see consistency across the books of the *Politics* rather than acknowledging the development of arguments. Sensitivity to this development is especially important when we consider how the passage from Book 1 concerning the political animal that is man becomes problematic as we proceed through the treatise. It is particularly by focusing on the place of democracy in Aristotle's analysis that we come to understand its problematic nature. We must recognize in Aristotle the willingness to pose puzzles for his readers, with the resolutions to those puzzles never as clear-cut as they may at first seem. Indeed, the puzzles often become far more complex as Aristotle explores underlying claims and consequences.

By the time Aristotle writes, the word "democracy" is no longer a stranger in the language of Attic Greek. Herodotus barely used the term, it was infrequent in Thucydides, but with Plato and Aristotle in the fourth century it is clearly the term applied to the regime in which the many (*to plēthos*) rule by passing decrees in the assembly, however much Socrates in Book 8 may ignore, on purpose, this meaning of democracy. For Aristotle, as I shall argue, democracy begins by being the universal regime, the regime that incorporates his definition of man, the city, and the citizen. It is only through a consideration of the political implications of this "universal" regime that Aristotle comes to question the relationship between his original definition of the nature of man and the possibility of political justice. As with the other authors considered in this book, we must not attribute to Aristotle antidemocratic prejudices or aristocratic motivations. Rather, by reflecting on the nature of democracy and its multiplicity of forms, Aristotle captures the meaning of political life and whether—on its own terms—it provides for the life that is best for the human being.[1]

II

While equality as a concept is central to the role that democracy plays in the writings of Herodotus and Plato, we must begin our study of Aristotle with the recognition that equality for him applies to *all* regimes, not only democracy. Political equality is constructed, and each regime, be it democracy or oligarchy or aristocracy or even monarchy, defines who is equal and who is not. Though for many, Aristotle's notoriety derives from the reading of his work that makes him the exponent of a natural hierarchy, of the natural slave, of the "superiority" of the male to the female, the problem that this "natural hierarchy" poses for politics is that it is not easy for us to identify who *by nature* is superior to any other and therefore ought to have authority over another.

Already in the early passages of Book 1, Aristotle dismisses the legitimacy of "conventional" slavery, that which is against nature but is according to law (*para phusin, kata nomon*; 1253b20, 1255a5). This hierarchy is based only on force, having no foundation in nature, in the natural superiority of the master to the slave. Instead, Aristotle concentrates our attention on searching for the "natural" slave, the one who is like a tool, the one who produces rather than acts, the one who belongs to another human being, the one who benefits from being owned by another. To so benefit from being a slave, the possession of another man, though, one must be inferior in virtue and possess the body of a slave. But, again we encounter difficulties. What is such a body like and how do we know who is inferior in virtue since virtue is a quality of the soul? "It is not," Aristotle remarks, "as easy to see the beauty of the soul as that of the body" (1254b38–1255a1).[2] We sense here the difficulty of relying so readily on nature to guide us: "Nature wishes to make the body of the freeman and the slave different . . . but the opposite often happens, so that some have the bodies of free men and some the souls" (1254b27–34). And a few passages later he remarks on the assertion that good men should come from good men just as beasts are born from beasts: "Nature wishes to do this but often is unable to" (1255b3–4).

Since we cannot rely on nature to give us unambiguous assurances concerning who is superior and who is inferior, the political regime makes those distinctions, but having made them and offering definitions of equality and hierarchies, *para phusin, kata nomon*, these definitions, lacking any grounding in nature, will always be subject to debate; they will always be a source of instability in the regime, a source of conflict as members of the community disagree about the definitions of equality and inequality established by any particular regime. The potential for such debates, the destabilizing implications of such debates and what they tell us about the potential for justice in politics all play a major role in Aristotle's analysis of democracy. The issue for all political communities is to define who is equal precisely because nature has not given us the skills to recognize equals and those who are not equal. Our powers of observation do not give insight into the souls of individuals such that we can know who is noble and who is base, who is good and who is bad. Democracies turn to numbers as the basis for authority and "superiority," but even here the debate arises: Who is to count in the calculation of numbers?

This complication arises because there are many dimensions along which one can define equality. Virtue, wealth, and free birth, two citizen parents or one, gender, blond hair are only a few.[3] Each of the criteria defines who is equal, and that in turn gives structure to a different regime, with different institutions. The typologies with which I sometimes express impatience are indeed critical, since each regime depends on a distinct definition of who is equal. The hierarchical world of male and female, master and slave, better and worse, soul and body may exist by nature, but it resists easy discovery. Thus Aristotle, the exponent of a hierarchical worldview, points out the inadequacy of all attempts to put this principle of hierarchy into practice in political life. Instead of following a hidden nature, we in political life construct our own equalities and inequalities, according to visible criteria that tell us nothing about what is in agreement with nature. And precisely because we cannot discover natural equalities with ease, we have intense debates about who is equal, who rules in the city, and who is ruled. These debates entail the crux of political life and the foundations of political regimes; they bring about revolutions, the movement from one regime to another in the very unstable world of political life.

In Book 2 of the *Politics*, Aristotle considers a variety of different regimes, some of which are in use by different cities that are said to be well ruled (*eunomeisthai*, 1260b30) and certain others that are "spoken of by certain individuals and seem to be well [structured]" (1260b31–32). Among those regimes imagined or "spoken of" is one proposed by a certain Phaleas. Aristotle's discussion of this regime gives us a sense of how he addresses the problematic nature of equality and the attempts to institutionalize different conceptions of equality. Aristotle had begun the discussion in Book 2 by noting that all communities entail sharing—the question is what and how much. Socrates had proposed sharing wives, children, and property to reduce the potential for conflict, but Aristotle complains that this turns the city into an individual and creates the setting for numerous acts of impiety (Book 2, chap. 2–5).[4] Phaleas argues that the greatest conflicts arise concerning property. To address this problem he does not propose that property be held in common as in Socrates' city, but that the possessions (*ktēseis*) of the citizens be equal (*isas*, 1266a40). To institute equality, Phaleas looks to a quality that is not subjective like beauty or virtue; he turns to what is quantifiable, namely, wealth. Thus, Phaleas (and, as Aristotle reminds us, Plato too in the *Laws*) proposed founding a new regime in which all citizens are equal with regard to their possessions; the city thus founded institutionalizes an equality that focuses on wealth, not virtue, not education. If one is legislating for a city already in existence, one could ensure equality of possessions through the careful manipulation of dowries.

Aristotle finds little to praise in Phaleas' proposals, not because he opposes the notion of equality of possessions. Later on in the *Politics*, he will argue that inequality of wealth is one of the greatest sources of instability in regimes (1303b15–17), but to be equal in possessions accomplishes little. For one thing, it says little about whether the citizens are equal in poverty or equal in excessive wealth, each of which has its own difficulties; more important, Aristotle refuses to see the citizen as only an economic man concerned only about economic inequalities. Phaleas proposed economic equality because he wanted to rid cities of conflict, but Aristotle recognizes that conflict has many sources. "The human being is not unjust only for the sake of necessities," for which reason Phaleas proposes equality of property. "They steal . . . so that they can be happy and not be desirous of things" (1267a3–6). And in Aristotle's classic line: "One is not a tyrant in order not to be cold" (1267a14). These concerns do not even get to the very practical difficulties that Aristotle points to for one trying to equalize wealth, e.g., how does one ensure that all families have the same number of male offspring who will inherit shares equal to the shares of all other inheritors of wealth?

Aristotle acknowledges that regimes define their equals, but the definitions not based on nature will never provide stability or security for a people always ready to debate the principle of equality in their own regime. Phaleas' proposal, while well-intentioned in its eagerness to eliminate conflict, is naive in its failure to recognize how complex is the effort to institutionalize equality—of any sort. Plato in his playfulness identified the equality of democracy with apathy and toleration. Aristotle in his seriousness recognizes how the equality traditionally associated with democracy is by its very nature always the source of conflict and contention. His writings remind us that politics is a realm of conflict about the very foundations of order on which it is built. Since democracies are the regimes which proclaim a primary interest in equality, they are also the regimes in which debates about its meaning and content are most severe.

III

Having made it clear that equality is constructed, that the political regime (the *politeia*) is the definer of who is equal and who is not, along whatever criteria we (or the regime) may choose, but also remembering that all claims to equality are subject to question, Aristotle in Book 3 of the *Politics* offers the first of many definitions of democracy. Chapter 7 of Book 3 begins the famous six-part typology of regimes: the correct or "straight" (*orthoi*) ones that look to the common benefit (*koinon sumpheron*) and the deviations that look to the private concerns of the one, the few, or the many. The correct regime where the multitude rule for the "common benefit" is called by the common, shared (*koinon*) name of all regimes, *politeia*, usually translated "polity" in this context (1279a37–39). Its deviation is democracy, which is rule for the advantage of the many rulers.

At first, Aristotle's definitions seem to make political analysis and typologies easy for us. It is only as he proceeds to consider the assertions he has made that the difficulties in his analysis arise. Democracy is the rule of the many, but having said this, he continues: democracy is *really* the rule of those without resources, the *aporoi*, the poor. Unfortunately, in most cities those without resources are the majority. We see at once that we cannot take Aristotle's first definitions as decisive. He began his analysis with a typology that focused on numbers and the common benefit, but in the very next chapter he questions that typology by moving to an economic rather than numerical definition of democracy. Aristotle poses for himself the counterfactual: What if the poor were in fact a minority and the rich a majority? If the wealthy majority ruled, Aristotle affirms this would still be an oligarchy, thereby explicitly changing the category along which his typologies were originally built from numbers to resources. We come quickly to recognize that Aristotle's typology of regimes depends on the qualities of who is considered equal and given a share of political power rather than on how many individuals rule in a particular city.[5]

We are unlikely to be satisfied with Aristotle's definition of democracy as the rule of the poor in their own self-interest. We would hardly be applauding the democratization of Eastern Europe and the former Soviet Union if all it meant were that the poor were to rule in their self-interest instead of the rich (or the Communist party) doing so. Obviously, we must go beyond Aristotle's initial definition, and while he begins with this definition of democracy, he himself takes us well beyond to show instead democracy as the universal regime, the regime that captures the nature of politics more effectively than all the others, but which as a result also points more to the limits than to the possibilities of politics—and thus raises questions about the relationship of what he says is "by nature" and political life. By analyzing democracies and what they can and cannot accomplish, by making democracy's "opposite" the "polity," the regime known by the generic name for regime, Aristotle qualifies for us the claims he makes for political life earlier in the work.

Near the beginning of the *Politics* Aristotle writes in the often quoted passage that the human being is a political animal by nature. To live outside the city is either to be less than human, a form of beast like the one-eyed monster the Cyclops who lives "without clan, without laws, without hearth" (1253a5), or to be more than human, to be divine. The special attribute that identifies us as human and as political is our capacity to speak, to reason, to engage in intellectual speculation; this is our *logos*. As Aristotle explains, the *logos* enables us to "make clear the advantageous and the harmful, and likewise the just and unjust" (1253a14–15). The human being as distinct from all other creatures carries on discourse about the good and the bad, about the choices he or she shall make.[6] The self-sufficiency of the god requires no choice; the beast, insensitive to issues of good and bad, just and unjust, makes none.

The venue in which humans debate the good and the bad, the harmful and the advantageous, in which they exercise their *logos* and do not simply respond to instincts focused on the acquisition of economic necessities and the production of offspring, is the city, the polis with its courts and offices and assemblies. This brief section describing human nature, coming close to the very beginning of the *Politics*, explains why the city is according to nature (*phusei*, 1253a1). The city is not natural because it arises simply by nature as, e.g., a flower springs from a bulb or an acorn, fallen on the forest floor, becomes an oak tree. The human being as political by nature makes choices according to reason and the city itself is the result of choices, choices about which regimes one shall enjoy, about who even is to be made a citizen (1275b26–34). The polis is natural because the human being is more than a surviving, reproducing creature (1280a34). Human nature demands the city since without the city we cannot be human and reach our *telos* or end as creatures with *logos*. If we did not exercise our *logos*, we would not reach our *telos*; we would be no more than beasts and, as he says, the worst of beasts, "armed" as we are with the ability to be unjust as well as just (1253a34).

When Aristotle says at the start of this section on the political animal that "the end is nature [*hē de phusis telos estin*]" (1252b32), he is not simply offering a descriptive comment. He is making a normative statement; we ought to attain our goals, fulfill our nature. The acorn ought to become an oak tree and the child an adult. Should they not, some perversion of nature has taken place. To be political by nature also means in Aristotle's analysis that we ought to engage in politics lest we remain no more than the beasts, lest we fail to achieve our *telos/phusis*. We should raise the possibility at this point of a city which does not provide the venue for the human being to exercise his (or her) reason, for "living well," that for the sake of which we live in cities. Is such a city according to nature? Would these cities be comprised of slaves and animals—those less than human who do not have or use *logos*? These questions will haunt us when Aristotle considers democracy later in the work and concludes that the best democracy is the one with the least participation in the assembly.

At the beginning of Book 3, though, Aristotle turns to the generic regime and begins by asking the generic question: "What in the world is the city [polis]?" (1274b33–34). He does not ask what is a regime, what is Athens, what is a democracy, or an oligarchy, or an aristocracy. To answer his own question he says we must break down the city into its parts. And what are its parts? Not the buildings, not the sections of land, not the laws, not the individual classes of people, but the individual citizens, the human beings (or a particular set of human beings, as we learn in a moment) who, he has told us in Book 1, are political by nature. Since the part of the city we must study is the citizen, Aristotle then asks the obvious question: "Who is the citizen?" About this there is much debate (*amphisbēteitai*, 1275a2). The answer is not obvious, but Aristotle proposes a definition: "The citizen in an unqualified sense [*haplōs*] is defined by no other thing so much as sharing in judgments [*kriseōs*] and office [*archēs*]" (1275a22–23). Just a bit further down in the same passage, in a somewhat revised version of the definition, Aristotle now defines the citizen as "one for whom there is the freedom [*exousia*] to share in the offices [*archēs*], deliberation [*bouleutikēs*], and judging [*kritikēs*] of the city" (1275b18–19).

The two definitions differ in a way that is important in the later discussions of various types of democracies. The first definition, that the citizen is defined by no other thing so much as sharing in the judgments and offices of the city, is what we may call an active definition of citizenship, entailing direct participation in the political life of the city, but it omits the assembly and the deliberation that goes on in it. The second definition, that emphasizes the freedom to share in those activities and includes deliberations (presumably in the assembly), could be called the passive definition of citizenship. The opportunity for participation exists, but there is no requirement that the opportunity be exercised. Herein Aristotle seems to express the two models of citizenship that dominate contemporary debates in democratic theory and that authors such as M. I. Finley and Cynthia Farrar find are separated by two and a half millennia:[7] the active citizenry of ancient Athens versus the apathetic modern citizens who do not exercise the opportunity to share in the judgments, offices, or deliberations of the city.

Aristotle uses both definitions, however, to describe his generic citizen who is the key definitional unit of the generic city. The city provides the locus in which this citizen building-block can be human, where he lives well, exercising *logos* by judging and making choices concerning the good and the bad, the just and the unjust, the advantageous and the harmful, for otherwise the city would be made up of slaves or animals (1280a32–33). These two definitions, the "active" as well as the "passive," however, are only appropriate when we define the citizen as a citizen of a democracy. The city is, Aristotle concludes after defining the citizen, "a *plēthos* of such individuals sufficient for living self-sufficiently, to speak simply" (1275b20–21). The attempt to discover what in the world the city in general is at the beginning of Book 3 reduces to discovering—through the citizen—what in the world a democracy is.

In the consideration of the six-part typology that follows

Aristotle's examination of who is the citizen, we see the difficulty of applying this definition of citizenship to regimes other than democracy. But more important, he goes beyond the definition of the citizen, and in Chapter 10 of Book 3 he poses a major problem—or *aporia*, as he phrases it—of who ought (*dein*) to have authority (*kurion*) in the city (1281a11).[8] Aristotle answers this *aporia* with a proposed list of potential candidates that includes the many, the wealthy, the "best" one, and the tyrant. All the offered answers pose problems (*duskolia*, 1281a14), for the many and the wealthy are indeed no better than tyrants acting on the basis of force for their own self-interest.[9] In this rejection of the legitimacy of the various claimants to political authority in the city, the question arises of whether the "seemly [*to epieikes*]" (1281a28) should be given the authority. Aristotle responds that this too is not without problems for it deprives all the others (presumably the "unseemly"?) of the honors of political office. The attractiveness of having the best man or men (the "seemly") rule is moderated by the understanding of what it is to be human, namely, to share in the "honor" of political office. The city is according to nature so that the political animal can be a citizen, fill the offices, use his *logos*, and make choices, and yet the claims to give authority to one group or another, the majority, the few, the best, all lead to founding the city on the extreme of injustice or tyranny. "Whatever actions the tyrant does are necessarily entirely just. Being the strongest, he uses force just as the many with regard to the wealthy" (1281a22–24), or, we can add, the implied "wealthy with regard to the many."

While the difficulties of founding any regime on any legitimate basis besides force emerges most vividly in the *aporiai* of Book 3, Chapter 10, there are further objections to the many having authority, and while Aristotle begins with arguments about collective action, he is not averse to articulating those objections in the next chapter. Yet, he ultimately concludes in a noncommittal way that, justly (*dikaiōs*), the greater part (*to plēthos*) has authority or mastery (*kurion*) over most things (1282a38). To take us to this point Aristotle emphasizes the aggregation of good qualities: the more individuals there are to judge, the more likely it is that the judgments will be good; the more individuals there are involved in making laws, the better the laws are likely to be. There are advantages to having the many rule and it is "just" for *to plēthos* to have authority, but he concludes this discussion suddenly with an appeal to correctly enacted law rather than to the many (1282b8–13). Though a questionable justice that gives authority to an arbitrarily defined set of equals may turn that authority over to *to plēthos*, it is not clear that this ambiguous justice is the most politically desirable. The tension between law, *nomos*—that which rules irrespective of the decisions of the many, that which has authority whether decreed by the people or not—and democratic decree (*psēphisma*)—that which is determined by the force of the many—is one that keeps surfacing throughout Aristotle's work. There are a variety of concerns that affect our assessment of political regimes. Political justice may require granting authority to the many, but it may also come from the peaceful quiet of apathetic citizens working their farms rather than attending the assembly.

Despite his assertion at 1282a38 that, justly (*dikaiōs*), the many have mastery over most things, Aristotle keeps returning to the question of which group of equals—the many, the wealthy, the virtuous—has the just claim to rule. He keeps returning to the question because he finds it impossible to adjudicate between the claims, concluding once again that within the city the benefit of the whole must be attended to and again that the citizen, as "commonly understood [*koinēi*]," is one who shares in ruling and being ruled (1283b42–1284a1). He adds that how this is manifest will differ with each regime, but there is always the insistence that the citizen be willing to be *ruled* as well as to rule. This insistence raises the issue of the "god among humans" (1284a10–11), the one for whom it would be foolish or laughable (*geloios*) to establish limiting laws. For just this reason, democratically run cities have set up ostracism, to expel the "god among humans." What matters for the political community, then, is *not* that the best rule, since the best cannot, without being ridiculous, be ruled. This may not be best for the city as a whole: it is best to be ruled by the one best suited to rule over others as a god, but given the definition of the human being and of the citizen as one who shares in ruling and being ruled, the rule of the best does not allow for the political arena where we as humans can fulfill our natural human potential, attain our *telos*. There now appears a contradiction between what is best for the whole and what allows for the fulfillment of the nature of the many. Nature gives mixed signals: there is the natural hierarchy of the superior over the inferior (as in a city without citizens, namely, a monarchy of a godlike man) and then there is the human being achieving his or her *telos* as the political animal exercising *logos* by making choices in the political realm.

Kingship, nevertheless, the apolitical regime, intrigues the tireless Aristotle. Though kingship may assert a natural hierarchy, Aristotle has defined kingship out of politics. Yet he concludes the third book of the *Politics* with an extended reflection on the various types of kingship. In the midst of this discussion, however, he proposes a history of regimes, beginning with the rule of the best and moving to the rule of the many who are virtuous and to the decline into oligarchies, tyrannies, and finally into democracies. Democracy appears here as the final stage of this natural historical development of regimes, a conclusion further emphasized by Aristotle's comment that "since it has turned out that cities are larger, perhaps not easily does any other regime besides democracy come into being" (1286b20–22). Just as democracy becomes the only regime that adequately captures the definition of the citizen as the participant or the one who has the freedom to participate, so too democracy becomes the final regime, the one to which a history of regimes leads us and the one which the natural growth in size of cities has now made necessary. Even if we cannot assert the unambiguous justice of placing authority in the many (whose claim of numbers is no better than the tyrant's claim to power), nature and history appear to confirm the universality of democracy, democracy as the generic regime for the generic citizen, the regime that occurs at the end of the generic history of regimes.[10] It is, however, precisely this generic role that allows democracy also to illustrate the limits of politics as Aristotle explores further what he means by the city, the citizen, and justice.

IV

With democracy as the universal regime, the one that incorporates the broadest definition of the citizen and arises because of the natural historical developments as cities grow, Aristotle explores extensively, especially in Books 4 and 6, what this regime is, its types, and its relationship to its "opposite." As we proceed through the *Politics* Aristotle begins to leave behind the concern with the insoluble puzzle of the justice of the various claims to rule. He recognizes that the problem, incapable of resolution, leads to unending conflict and debate. Instead, he turns to the endurance of regimes, and the assessment of democracy and oligarchy comes to focus not on the question of justice but on that of stability. As a result, Aristotle points to the limits of the democratic regime if we focus on the assembly, on the power of the many and their authoritative status in the city. Abandoning the partial justice that is all political regimes can offer, we come to worry about whether the natural necessity of the human being as a political animal works against the stability of the regime sought in Book 4.

Aristotle often stops his discourse to inform us that he is writing for the one who will found, improve, preserve political regimes (*ho politikos*, 1289a6–7).[11] Such a one cannot be ignorant,

Aristotle tells us, of how many (*posa*) forms (*eidē*) of regimes there are, not just the original six of Book 3's typology, but the varieties now especially of democracy and oligarchy. Whereas in Book 3, democracy and polity were opposites, we now learn that democracy and oligarchy are the relevant opposites, just as the north wind is the opposite of the south wind. Oligarchy and democracy are the primary forms (*eidē*) and, as opposites, all else is simply a variation on these two, just as all winds are variations on the north wind and the south wind (1290a13–16). And so we learn of the multiple variations of democracy.

These variations arise because a city is composed of disparate parts and those parts can be joined in a variety of ways to create a variety of *politeiai*, regimes. We have the farmers, the merchants, the warriors, the artisans, the fishermen, the laborers, indeed also the wealthy and the poor. How each one overlaps with others (e.g., the farmers and the warriors) and which ones predominate determine the texture of each of these democracies. But the forms of democracies derive from who is included in the ruling group, who constitutes the authoritative element, whether the poor and the wealthy both participate, whether participation depends on a low monetary assessment, whether descent defines participation, and so forth. As Aristotle goes through this list of differences in terms of who is considered equal and who participates, and after asserting that a democracy is where the people (the *dēmos*) are the greater number and their opinion has authority, he once again suddenly introduces the rule of law as an important qualifier of what we mean by democracy and its types. "Another form of democracy is where whoever is of unquestioned descent shares in all the offices, but the law rules [*archein de ton nomon*]" (1292a1–2). Aristotle returns to the distinction between regimes in which the people as a multitude rule by decrees (*psēphisma*) and those in which the *nomoi*, the traditional rules and historical patterns of interaction, control the life of the city; where current speech backed by an adequate number of hands in the assembly becomes the law, in contrast to the regime in which the voice of the assembly is severely limited by the past, by historically grounded assertions about what ought and ought not to be done. In the former, communal decision-making is of the moment and unrestrained; in the latter, communal decision-making is set into the context of the past and thereby very much constrained.

Without question Aristotle prefers the democratic regime in which the laws rather than the assemblies, with their decrees backed by the force of numbers, rule. Some, like Sheldon Wolin, would say this is undemocratic (1994);[12] others praise the ancient "republic" in which this was the case (e.g., Sealey 1987). In Aristotle's view, the exercise of authority by assemblies is tyrannical. As he had said in Book 3, Chapter 10, "[the tyrant] being strong uses force, just like *to plēthos* with regard to the wealthy" (1281a22–23). In addition he now notes that the rule of assemblies allows for the rise of the demagogues like Alcibiades. More significantly, though, through their very participation in the assembly, the people become a monarch (*monarchos gar ho dēmos ginetai*, 1292a11, 15); the people lose their individuality: "The many are in authority not as individuals [*hōs hekatos*], but all together" (1292a12–13). To use what is perhaps too-contemporary language, democracy as the rule of the assembly, according to Aristotle here, destroys autonomy rather than enhancing it.

Once Aristotle has made the analogy to the monarchy, it is but a short step to tyranny, or the tyranny of the assembled people. Comparing the demagogues who arise in such a democracy to the flatterers of a tyrant, he castigates them precisely because they enable decrees to become authoritative over the traditional laws. When this happens, "all offices are overthrown" (1292a29–30) and the assembly rules. Thus, while humans may be political animals, a political regime in which the assembly rules through its decrees, even though voted upon by the many, revealing their judgments about the good and the bad, the just and the unjust, the advantageous and the harmful, is opposed to what is natural, the hierarchy of the better over the inferior. As in Book 3, Chapter 10, the rule of the many is always subject to question. The tension continues between the hierarchical structure of nature and the human *telos* of the political animal. The challenge that Aristotle sets for democracy is whether the two demands of nature can be combined and reconciled or whether nature has in some sense abandoned us to chose one or the other.

On further reflection, Aristotle goes so far as to claim that the democracy in which the assembly rules is not a regime at all, for where the traditional laws do not rule, there can be no *politeia* (1292a32).[13] It is without order and structure, varying according to the whims of a tyrannical assembly. It is necessary, Aristotle continues, "that the traditional laws rule over all things, while the offices and the regime judge each particular" (1292a33–34). Aristotle, as in many places in the *Politics*, seems to be leading us in a series of concentric circles, leaving us often more confused than Socrates does in his explicitly aporetic dialogues. But the thrust of Aristotle's argument here seems to be that the simple participation by the poor in the assembly passing decrees does not make the city democratic. The assembly is not the central institution in defining a democracy. Or, as Aristotle phrases it: "If democracy is one of the regimes, it is clear that such a one in which decrees [*psēphisma*] control all things is not a democracy properly" (1292a34–36).[14]

To the degree that voting on decrees is all that one does, one is not a participant in a polis, one is not attaining one's nature as a political animal. We must remember that Aristotle's definition of a citizen mentioned first the *necessity* to participate in offices and law courts: only as an afterthought was the "opportunity" or "freedom" to participate in deliberation mentioned. The assembly is not mentioned at all in the first definition of a citizen nor is the assembly what defines a democracy for Aristotle. Indeed, as Aristotle suggests in Book 4, reliance on the assembly is the absence of a regime, and in Book 6 he suggests that that regime is perhaps best in which the assembly is least attended.

What conditions, then, give rise to a democracy in the proper sense rather than to a regime that is not a democracy but a tyranny ruled by the decrees of the assembly? Here as elsewhere in the *Politics*, Aristotle proceeds to praise a democracy that is based on farmers who have only moderate amounts of money. When such individuals as these are in authority in the city, they rule according to laws. They need to spend their time farming and do not have the leisure to spend time attending frequent meetings of the assembly. "Setting the law [*ton nomon*] in charge, they assemble only for necessary assemblies" (1292b28–29). Or if the democracy, while open to all of a certain parentage, let us say, or all who are free, offers no pay to those who attend the assembly, then this regime will also be ruled by law; only those who have the leisure to attend can share in authority.

We need not here interpret Aristotle as a conservative displaying "gentlemanly contempt for the lower classes" as Neal and Ellen Wood would claim (1978, 215). Rather, the less participation in the assembly generally, the better for the city as a whole. The assembly making a claim to rule on the basis of numbers is inherently unjust, legitimizing itself on no surer basis than the tyrant. To worry that the assembly has authority is to worry about tyrannical foundations for political rule, not necessarily about personal qualities of the potential attendees at the assembly. Aristotle, as Plato before him, considers activity in the assembly hazardous to the health of a city. The better the democracy, the less frequent and the less important the assembly.[15]

Aristotle imagines a democracy attaining its "final" or complete state (*teleutia*) when it has grown large and can import resources. But this final democracy is not a blessing; with significant external resources flowing into the city, the many become sufficiently rich to have time to attend the assembly. With that widespread attendance, decrees rather than traditional laws rule.

Thus, democracy deteriorates into the feared tyranny of numbers, and the multitude, not the laws, have authority. Democracy, the generic regime with the generic citizen, by its very nature, degenerates into a tyranny of the whole. We are left with the problem of what regime does not so decline. Does there exist by nature a regime in which men and women can be the political animals Aristotle has said they are by nature, without having them become part of the tyrannical whole?

V

Anyone who has read Aristotle beyond the famous quotes about the political man and the definition of a citizen knows that the regime that he calls by the generic term "polity" in Book 3 raises questions about the neat typologies that Aristotle had introduced following his definition of the citizen. Polity here is not the "opposite" of democracy, but a mixture of democracy and oligarchy, a blending together of wealth and poverty, resources and the absence of resources. He had called polity one of the "straight [*orthoi*]" regimes, the opposite of democracy.[16] As the analysis proceeds, it becomes clear that its status as one of the good regimes in the original typology is blurred. It is now praised not because its rulers attend to the interest of the whole city; in fact, it is clear that they attend to their private interests. It receives praise because it offers stability, although perhaps not justice. Indeed, justice, independent of a particular regime's definition of equality, we must come to understand, cannot be the goal of politics. This would require the rule of the best, which in turn means the demise of political life. Since the political regime cannot achieve that absolute justice, we may need to lower our goals and aim for stability, a reasonable stability, which nevertheless allows for a certain degree of political activity for the political animal.

The process of mixing the regime of oligarchy with democracy into polity for the sake of stability uncovers, though, some of Aristotle's reservations about democracy as practiced at Athens.

He suggests, for example, that officers in a city be chosen, i.e., selected by a vote or by some other mechanism which entails the making of judgments. This requires the evaluation of individuals rather than the assigning of office by lot or chance. The issue again is the question of why politics in the first place? To live well, is the answer, not just to live, because the human being is the only animal with *logos*, the capacity to choose. Relying on lot is an abdication from choice, an abdication from politics, an abdication from living well. At the same time that Aristotle rejects lot as the basis for political office, he likewise emphasizes that wealth is not to serve as a criterion. To rely on wealth as a determining factor as to who should serve in the offices of the city in no way ensures that the process of selection entails the reasoning faculty either. It is perhaps no more than relying on lot, the chance distribution of wealth among the members of the city.[17]

Lacedaemonia achieves the balance that Aristotle argues is appropriate. In Lacedaemonia, there is no discrimination according to wealth: "Not at all are the rich man and the poor man distinguishable from the other" (1294b26), neither in their education nor in where they eat. But discrimination or selection does enter the polis when offices are to be filled; in contrast to Athenian courtrooms of several hundred judges, in Lacedaemonia "a few have authority over death and exile" and, as Aristotle phrases it in his casual way, "other things of the sort" (1294b33–34). Aristotle wants limits on participation in the regime, but wealth is not the right basis on which to set those limits. Limits may be necessary for stability and to prevent a tyranny of the whole, but these limits cannot be justified by criteria that take no account of the worth of the individual who is or is not to hold political office. Nevertheless, the very praise of the limits on participation reinforces the contradiction between the original claim that man is a political animal and where we find ourselves in Book 4. Lot allows for anyone to participate, to live the good life using his or her reflective reason, but at the same time relying on the lot to fill the offices means that there is no exercise of reflective judgment in the assigning of offices.

Though Aristotle asks at the beginning of Book 4 about what life is possible for most people to share, he emphatically does not envision the participation of the many in the best possible practical regime. He instead turns to those in the middle, those who have neither too much nor too little. To have too much means that one does not know how to be ruled, while those who have too little know least of all how to rule, and yet are eager to rule. Both, not knowing how to be ruled and being eager for rule, create a city of masters and slaves, the former scornful of those who are inferior, the latter jealous of those who have power. If there is a large group in the middle with neither too much nor too little there will be neither arrogance nor jealousy. Thus, they would desire to rule neither too much nor too little. In such a regime, with a large middle class, there would be the absence of conflict, and in this context the bigger city is freer of faction than a smaller one, Aristotle argues, because the middle part will be the most numerous. All these are empirical claims, subject to the analyses of our contemporary social scientists, but in the process of posing these assertions about the problematic effects of a large middle class, Aristotle, in these middle books of the *Politics*, moves beyond the goal of the fulfillment of human potential through participation in the political life of the city to a concern with the democratic regime that is most likely to be stable.

Now democracy receives approval not because it is in accord with the nature of the political animal, but because democracy is more likely to have more of the middle sort than oligarchy and, therefore, is likely to be more stable than oligarchy. This favorable notice is given with a view to the endurance of the regime rather than to its role as leading to the achievement of the human end or *telos*. At one point Aristotle concludes, and usually, we must remember, Aristotle does not "conclude"; he puzzles. Nevertheless, he concludes: "Where the multitude of the middling class predominates over both extremes or even over one, there will be a lasting regime" (1296b38–40). But at the same time, he warns us that though this may be the best practical regime, it has either never arisen or has done so infrequently.

As Aristotle reads the poor, they do not want participation; they want to be left alone, not forced to attend assemblies or to fight when they do not have the resources to do so. The challenge, though, is for the political leaders concerned with the stability of their regimes to prevent those who do possess the honors and the offices from creating a situation in which the poor will want power. We see, throughout this section of the *Politics*, the struggling Aristotle: on the one hand, he has defined the human being as a political animal; on the other, he cares about the preservation of the stable political community. The contradictions pervade: to fulfill human nature is to jeopardize the regime in which human nature is fulfilled. To participate is to threaten the stability of the regime in which one participates. As in the case of the bodies of slaves and masters which are never easy to identify, nature does not always make life easy for us, giving us goals that themselves may undermine the mechanism established to achieve those goals. Indeed, nature often leaves us confused and caught in a variety of self-contradictory situations, and it is the democratic regime that most vividly highlights these contradictions.

While Aristotle is not eager for the poor to participate because of the threat of democratic tyranny, he also recognizes that they, the poor, are necessary if the city is to be defended. Thus the poor must be part of the city in order to defend it, even if they are not participants in the offices and the law courts. The craft of the statesman, it seems, is to make the poor share in the city, but not share in its rule. In Book 4 Aristotle's proposal to meet this challenge is not to exclude the poor, but to draw the wealthy into the governing process by doing what is done in oligarchies with regard to the courts, to set fines for nonattendance. "All deliberating," he says, "now will deliberate better in common, the demos along with the notables and the notables along with the many" (1298b19–21). The assembly is not for open discussion, for engagement in discourse about the good and the bad, but becomes here a mechanism or half-truth publicly proclaimed (*prophasis*)[18] that is devised (*sophizontai*) by which the many "share" in the *politeia* (1297a14). The assembly curiously is instrumental in the survival of the city because it can transform the many into warriors, ready to defend the city and preserve it against external threats, not because it satisfies the needs of a political animal.

Book 5 offers a somewhat different solution. Here Aristotle envisions the apathetic many who have no desire to rule but wish to remain attentive to their private affairs (*tois idiois*, 1309a4–6);[19] they will be aroused to participation or involvement only if they think that those who hold political office are reaping unwarranted financial benefits. If there appears to be no profit from holding office, the poor will not wish to rule and will prefer to spend their time on their own affairs. Those who are already wealthy have no need to take advantage of the public funds, so the challenge is to get them to participate. Aristotle argues that honors for political power on its own have no particular attraction for such men who would gladly—like the poor—avoid the responsibilities of political participation. Aristotle has turned us around. Though by nature, he told us early in his treatise, the human being is a political animal, we want the many to be busy with their private affairs and we must bribe the wealthy with honors to get them to participate in what ought to be the natural activity for the human being, or we must use the assemblies as a "trick" to get the poor to be devoted to the city.

The democratic ideal of a participatory regime of active debate by men—rich or poor—seeking immortality through speech is left far behind as the analysis considers the economic substructure of wealth and poverty underlying political institutions of the regimes of ancient Greece. With the goal now stability, democracy appears preferable to oligarchy as the more stable of the two. A democracy where "the middle" is strong is preferable to one where "the middle" cannot act as a moderating force between the wealthy and the poor. Aristotle had begun his discussion of democracy as one of the six types of *politeiai* or regimes. He then asked the question of who should have power / authority (*kurion*) in the regime; all answers were unsatisfactory, reducing to either a tyrannical exercise of power or the exclusion of the citizen from participation in the life for which he was formed by nature. All proposals for the distribution of authority in regimes are ambiguous. In Book 6 again, Aristotle explicitly engages in the discussion of democracies in which assemblies meet often. These assemblies tend to be tyrannical and function in opposition to established law, leading to the expropriation of the wealth of others. Further, attendance at assemblies takes time from economic development. The discussion of democracy as "authority of the many" leads to much discomfort in Aristotle's analysis. We cannot really distinguish between an assembly and a tyrant; neither has a claim to authority based on anything besides power—and furthermore, political involvement leads to economic decline.

Contemporary democratic theory, as noted in the first chapter of this book, heavily influenced by Rousseau's general will and citizens as the makers of the laws that govern them, focuses on the "assembly" or what we would today call the legislature where, for example, Congress is the mechanism for expressing the sovereignty of the people, for determining the "will" of the majority, for accommodating the interests of the whole. Aristotle's discussion illustrates the tensions raised by this focus on democracy as collective decision-making and suggests how this process can easily be construed as no better than a tyrannical claim to rule based on power or force. Aristotle's discussion of democracy rather turns us to the original generic definition of the generic citizen, the one who simply partakes in the judgments and the offices of the city. It is as such that the human being is a political animal, judging, choosing, exercising *logos*. It is this political animal who lives a life distinct from that lived by beasts, by the man-eating Cyclops, and by the gods. Insofar as democracies focus on the opportunities for citizens to fulfill their humanity through these activities, they may be "by nature." Insofar as they search for some collective sovereignty of the people, aggregated preferences, general wills, and so forth, they have no more foundations in a natural justice than the tyranny of Book 3, Chapter 10.

We need not consider Aristotle for or against democracies; statements taken from his writings at random show him to be both. Nor need we express dismay at his preference for democracies where assemblies meet only infrequently. Rather, we should attend to how he alerts us to the potential injustices of such regimes at the same time that he also clarifies how democracy properly structured is the only regime in which the human being, individually rather than collectively, can fulfill his or her human potential. Autonomy, self-rule, is not the issue for Aristotle; engagement is. The autonomy associated with assemblies may lead to threats of tyranny. The political animal we are by nature does not.

Epilogue

We need not attribute to the ancient Athenians a Rousseauian vision of the social contract, see them as Arendt did, as seeking immortality through public speech, or extol their vision of freedom as I. F. Stone did, in order to marvel at that first attempt to institutionalize the principle of equality through the assembly, through the sharing of offices, through the use of the lot to assign those offices. The achievement of the Athenians is perhaps worthy of some of the mythmaking that has attended ancient democracy over the last century and a half. With the work of our contemporary historians we are now in a far better position to assess how that democracy actually functioned, what successes it had in carrying out this institutionalized equality, and what limits were placed on its accomplishments.

I have tried in this volume to explore what the ancient theorists who observed the emerging democratic regime in the fifth century and its more mature expression in the fourth found of significance in this institutionalized equality. This has entailed confronting a tradition that has looked upon most of the ancient theorists, with the possible exception of Herodotus, as elitists, smug in their attitudes towards a regime that accorded political authority to the many. I have argued that to be so dismissive means the loss of their insights into the nature, presuppositions, benefits, and tensions of a democratic regime.

Herodotus began with a delight in the beauty of equality, giving his character Otanes a speech in which he says that *isonomia* is the most beautiful of names. But he recognized that equality may need to be the result of a human construction, that is, its beauty may not arise from nature but from the human distaste for inequality. And yet he also recognized that while equality may be beautiful, inequality may be necessary within a political regime. This need not be an inequality according to nature, but an inequality of authority that political regimes must construct. Behind both—the constructed equality and the constructed inequality—is the fundamental assertion, however, essential to the institution of the democratic regime, that political communities do not simply arise by nature. Herodotus' tale of the seven Persian conspirators and the proposals for monarchy, oligarchy, and *isonomia* captures what later social contract theorists recognized, namely, the regime is a matter of choice. To empower equality or to empower inequality is a decision of political founders, not a decree from heaven or nature. Herodotus, who so often in his *Histories* portrays the human being as a plaything of the gods and of fate, gives to men in the political realm a potency of creation that is part of a democratic assertion of control over our world rather than mere submission to it.

Herodotus' story of the Persians and their war with the Greeks touches only peripherally on the questions of democratic regimes. In Thucydides' *History* the central character, the city of Athens, is a democracy. His study must therefore address democratic institutions head-on. Instead of allowing ourselves to be commandeered by the rhetoric of Hobbes's praise of Thucydides' own praise of monarchy, we must note Thucydides' treatment of the assemblies not as vacillating, manipulable bodies of men but as opportunities for cities to reflect on past decisions, to revoke, to change, to assert an independence from history. In a world of uncertainty and chance, where demagogues are interested only in their own advancement, where rhetoric rather than reason can sway men, the assembly's capacity to reverse itself captures the beneficial effects of democratic regimes. The multiplicity of members, the change over time, the openness for debate in the assembly, all these provide the opportunity to change past decisions, to express an independence from the grip of history. This does not always happen; indeed, it does not often happen—perhaps it only happens when the gods send their gifts in the person of Diodotus—but the democratic assembly provides the primary venue in which it *can* happen.

Plato's Socrates gives us yet another spin on the exercise of political principles within democratic regimes. The democracy he imagines is not dangerous in and of itself, but its effects are the worst of all, namely, the emergence of the tyrant. It is not that democracy is tyrannical. It is, in fact, just the opposite. Rather democracy as the full expression of equality and freedom means a total tolerance of all—and thus an inability or a refusal to distinguish between good and bad, worthy and unworthy, beautiful and ugly. The failure to "discriminate" means that a certain apathy pervades the polity, an apathy that opens the door for the violence of tyranny.

It is Aristotle who goes so far as to make us recognize the theoretical equation of democracy and tyranny, not because of a haughty dismissiveness towards *to plēthos*, but because of the theoretical challenge of trying to distinguish between a majority that forcefully imposes its will, using sheer numbers as a justification, and the tyrant who likewise imposes his will simply because he has acquired a monopoly of force. By making this analogy Aristotle forces us to question whether there can ever be a just response to the question of who *ought* to have political authority. Numbers are not adequate to ensure justice for Aristotle. Nevertheless, while numbers do not give legitimacy, Aristotle's definition of the human being as neither beast nor god because of the human possession of *logos* relies on the opportunities that men create for themselves to exercise that *logos*. Through his study of democracy, he points to the inherent contradictions between the goals of justice and nature, appearing to urge in the end the abandonment of the search for justice in politics, emphasizing instead the fulfillment of human potential in the exercise of political action, albeit also recognizing the self-defeating quality of that involvement since increases in engagement—at least in the assembly—lead to increased instability.

Each of the authors discussed offers a different perspective on the democratic regime; there is no uniformity in their reactions to democratic principles and practices. They do not offer some coherent, unified democratic theory, but they give us instead some of the texture of democratic institutions that has too often been ignored in the emphasis on a sovereign people and general wills, elections and representation, in the contemporary assessments of democratic regimes. In the return to the ancients for our own beginning, we see the complexity of democracy's achievements and limits. By studying those complexities we gain far more than an ideological metaphor for what we choose to excoriate or praise.

Notes

Preface

1. Quoted in Reinhold (1984, 108), from the *Writings of Thomas Jefferson* IV, 65–66.

2. Indeed, since I began this book, a work dealing far more extensively with the "abuse" of ancient democracy has appeared with the title *Athens on Trial: The Antidemocratic Tradition in Western Thought*, by Jennifer Tolbert Roberts (1994). I regret that I was not aware of this work and its wealth of sources earlier. Incorporation of the material Roberts presents would have greatly enhanced my own arguments and presentation.

Chapter One: Mythmakers

1. Herodotus, according to most manuscripts, describes himself as coming from Halicarnassus and thus does not fit quite so easily into this grouping. Nevertheless, as he tells his stories of a multitude of regimes, he becomes perhaps the first author to observe seriously a democratic regime and thus gives us a sense of the principles underlying the commitment to the earliest democratic forms.

2. Emphasis added. The Modern Library edition with a translation by Crawley is far more accurate: "Its administration favors the many instead of the few; this is why it is called a democracy" (Thucydides 1982, 108). Even a scholar such as M. H. Hansen, whose scholarship has been

the foundation of contemporary study of Athenian democracy, translates Thucydides as saying, "The constitution is called democracy (demokratia) because rule is not by the few but by the majority" (1989, 3). It is satisfying to note that Robert Dahl's book *Democracy and Its Critics* uses the language of Crawley's translation rather than Warner's when he offers the portrait of Athenian democracy in the voice of a young Athenian interlocutor (1989, 17).

3. Even "administration" is too strong. The Greek word that Hobbes is translating here, *oikein*, entails caring for the household, for what is one's own.

4. See also Stockton (1990, 95), who argues that there was no conscious concern with representation. Rather, becoming a bit defensive, he asserts that the *boulē* and the courts were representative. "If we can nowadays regard the twelve randomly chosen members of a jury as in some sense representative of the community at large . . . we surely cannot deny the epithet 'representative' to the Athenian *boulē*." This is not the issue; the issue is whether the Athenians justify their regime in terms of representation, not whether we do. Much of the recent scholarship on the history of Athenian democracy does seem to point to far more limited participation on the part of citizens and thus expresses the worry about how to retain the title "democracy" for the regime at Athens. There are extremes such as Carter (1986), but Sinclair (1988) sounds a similar theme, while Whitehead (1986) focuses on participation on the local level. Osborne is more sanguine, suggesting: "It seems quite likely that perhaps 70% of Athenians over thirty served at least once" (1985, 237n. 56). He is generally positive about the democratic success in Athens: "All citizens did have access to the true centre of power, but indirectly, and the *access was all the more effective for being indirect*" (1985, 92, emphasis added to this curious and ambiguous final phrase.) Ober (1989a) is more concerned with the limits that the masses can put on the elite participants than on the participation of the many. See also Rhodes (1972).

5. Wood (1988) effectively debunks the notion that an idle mob comprised the citizen body at Athens and shows the origins of that view in an early ideological antidemocratic bias.

6. See the excellent review by Ober (1989b) of Hansen's book on just this point. Ober asks specifically whether Hansen has "posed

meaningful questions" (323) and in particular asks whether it is appropriate to use the language of "sovereignty" when talking about the ancient world (332).

7. For a full discussion of the democratic tone of Aeschylus' play, see Podlecki (1986).

8. See Farrar's extended discussion of this pasage (1988, 77–98). Farrar identifies Protagoras as "so far as we know, the first democratic political theorist in the history of the world" (77).

9. It is here that Roberts (1994) is a most valuable supplement to my presentation. She develops in far more detail than I am able to do here this "use" of Athenian democracy, and she includes the German response as well.

10. See also Miles (1974, 263) on how pervasive the language of Rome, rather than that of Athens, was during the founding period. Leaders then turned to the "Capitol," the "Senate," and called America "this embryo Rome." A recent publication (Richard 1994) which appeared since I gave these lectures makes a similar point about the preference for Rome and points to how the founders relied on the aristocratic critics of Athens, not on the defenders of Athenian democracy. Wills (1992, 42) refers us to the image of Washington as Cincinnatus and comments "[w]hen Jefferson laid out the plan for his University of Virginia, he fashioned everything to Roman architectural standards."

11. Reinhold (1984, 107) quotes a certain John Taylor, who rejected John Adams' praise of Sparta, saying it lacked a democratic balance and put its government in the hands of a minority, but Taylor was the exception.

12. Among the books that trace the growth of what has been called "the Greek fever" by the scholars of philhellenism and the sympathy for the Greeks fighting for liberation from the Turks are Cline (1930); Booras (1934); Dakin (1955); Long ([1935] 1963); Pappas (1985); Wills (1992).

13. Quoted in Bain (1873, 14) from Grote's review of Mitford's *History* in the April 1826 *Westminster Review*.

14. Quoted in Turner (1981, 208) from Grote's review of Mitford in the April 1826 *Westminster Review*.

15. Pangle (1988, 50) makes the criticism: "Her repeated celebrations of Pericles and Periclean Athens abstract from the imperialism that was

the heart of Periclean policy." See also Beiner's important qualification: "Arendt has very little confidence that reflection on ancient practice will, by itself, dissolve the perplexities of the present" (1990, 250).

16. Quoted in Finley (1973, 4).

17. It will also be obvious that I am less interested in discovering an author's political stance or attitude—for or against democracy—than I am in listening to what they have to say about the theoretical foundations of democracy. See, e.g., Stockton (1990, 167).

Chapter Two: Herodotus

1. Much attention has centered on the famous debate in Book 3 that sets democracy, oligarchy, and monarchy against each other. Though I will discuss this debate at the end of the chapter, I find that there has been far too much attention paid to this section and not enough to the other political issues that suffuse Herodotus' text.

2. Ehrenberg (1950, 517–24) argues for an earlier date through his analysis of the language of Aeschylus' first play, *Suppliant Women*, where he finds the juxtaposition of *plēthos* and *dēmos* and *archē* and *kratia* as indications that democracy was part of the political discourse considerably before the 440s. See however, Vlastos (1953, 338–39) for a response. Hansen (e.g., 1991, 69–70) disputes this and finds no evidence for the use of *isonomia* as the predecessor of *dēmokratia* at Athens.

3. *Eunomia*, in contrast to *isonomia*, was the seventh-century term associated with good rule; it means "good laws" or, drawing on its etymological roots, a good distribution. As Ehrenberg points out (1950, 532–33), Solon's regime was *eunomia*. "Distribution" here can be according to worth and may treat members of a city unequally. With the introduction of *isonomia* the emphasis moves to a focus on equality and perhaps equal distribution, not, however, in the sense of property but of the engagement with the laws of the city. Vlastos (1953, 348, 352) prefers "law" to "distribution" as the proper meaning of *nomos*. Vlastos points to the further importance of the *political*, rather than the economic, power that comes from *isonomia*. The focus is on institutions rather than possessions. For a discussion of the theoretical dimensions of *isonomia* see, among others, Euben (1978).

4. Sealey notes (1974, 253): "The conclusion will be that *dēmokratia* had only minimal value as a descriptive or empirical term; its force resided in its complex overtones of approval or disapproval, dissuasion or commendation, hate or love."

5. So much of the contemporary discomfort in talking favorably about ancient democracy comes from its exclusion of women, slaves, and metics. Our principles, which emphasize inclusion, make us resistant to understanding the ancient struggle with this problem from the opposite perspective, that of exclusion.

6. Benardete (1969, 122) comments as he begins to discuss the second half of the *Inquiries* (the title he gives to Herodotus' work): "Greece would appear to be nothing more than a digression from or an addition to the nature of things," though Benardete goes on to say that Herodotus, by devoting half of the work to Greece, is giving Greece a disproportionate share of attention.

7. Cicero first called Herodotus the "Father of History" (*Laws* 1.1.5).

8. This, of course, ignores the fact that the words "constitutional" and "government" are Latin, with no easy parallels in the Greek.

9. Flory (1987, 143–44) has the rather unfriendly reading of this passage as follows: "Herodotus feels he must explain in detail how democracy could result in military success, since this idea contradicts the theories current in his day; indeed, it runs counter to Demaratus' explanation of the success of the Spartans in battle because they obey *nomos* as a *despotēs*."

10. This is not to suggest that Herodotus does not recognize that medicine may be a science at which some excel; see his account of Democedes (3.130), whose knowledge of things medical is behind his own rise, first as doctor to Polycrates, and then to Darius.

11. Benardete (1969, 27) comments that it is Herodotus, not the Babylonians, who says which of their customs is the most beautiful and which the ugliest.

12. Hall (1989, 96) notes: "The composite verb *proskunein* is not found in Greek sources before the Persian wars." See also Momigliano (1979, 145–46).

13. How and Wells ([1912] 1989, 1:278) entitle this section of Herodotus' text "The Beginning of Greek Political Philosophy."

14. There is a later reference to the speech by Otanes as the one "praising democracy" (6.43). At 4.137 Histaeus says of the cities of Ionia, each one "prefers to be ruled by the demos [*dēmokrateesthai*] rather than by a tyrant [*turanneuesthai*]," but the word "tyrant" is used, not *basileus* (king).

15. Benardete makes the point (1969, 85) that this means a certain mediocrity, but Vlastos' appreciation of Otanes' speech is to my mind the most important. He finds it radical in that Otanes attributes bad government, not to vicious men, but to the institutions that give men power: "Otanes does not idealize the people's virtue. He does not claim that the people's rule will be good because the people are just and wise. He says only that their rule will be responsible and equal" (1953, 359).

Chapter Three: Thucydides

1. Since I wrote these lectures I have become aware of an article by Ober (1993) in which he explores Thucydides' understanding of what Ober calls "democratic knowledge." While Ober's approach and conclusions are somewhat different from mine, he does show an interest in learning about democracy from Thucydides rather than just portraying him as antidemocratic (though he sees him as that, too).

2. We should keep in mind, of course, how many deeds of how many men are entrusted to the speech of Thucydides.

3. See Pericles' first speech at 1.144.1 where he urges the Athenians not to add onto their empire (*archē*) while fighting.

4. Vernant in his highly schematized portrait of the development of democracy in Athens suggests an analogue between the citizen and the hoplite member of the phalanx where the role of each was the same: "The democratic current . . . defined all citizens, without regard to fortune or quality, as 'equals' having precisely the same rights to take part in all aspects of public life. . . . The problem was . . . to eliminate all the differences that had set the various parts of the city against one another, and to blend and merge them so that on the political level citizens were no longer differentiated in any respect" (1982,

97–98). Though schematized in Vernant, his model of citizenship is, I believe, captured vividly in Pericles' Funeral Oration.

5. This is in no way to suggest that the old hierarchy is preferable to the new hierarchy that abstracts from particularity, only to clarify how Thucydides helps us here understand that underlying the democratic institutions as conceived by Pericles is the abstraction from an attachment to particularities. The democracy he envisions is deracinating, though without eliminating hierarchy.

6. I will note below some of the analogies between Pericles' Funeral Oration and Socrates' account of the city of Callipolis, but here we might note how Socrates, in preparing his warriors for war, spends precious little time in Books 3 and 4 of the *Republic* addressing their physical training, and focuses on their education in music and poetry.

7. Gomme (1956, 2.166) comments that *elloionto* is in the pluperfect, suggesting that the controversy about the policy had begun before Pericles had returned from his expedition.

8. Gomme (1956, 2.166) wonders whether there was more than one ambassador sent because of the use of *tinas* after *presbeis*. That would indicate the seriousness of the "change of mind" that has taken place.

9. He did not do this earlier in the Book when the Athenians were agitatedly discussing whether to go out of the city to meet the attacking Spartan forces (see 2.22).

10. The same sentiment is repeated in 2.61: "The mind [*hē dianoia*] does not remain strong in what you know [*egnōte*]."

11. See further the discussion in Chapter 6 of Saxonhouse (1992).

12. In Book 1 we are not told of any dissenters after Pericles urges the Athenians to stand firm and face war, should it be the consequence of such a stance. With Pericles' assurances of economic independence, the Athenians of Book 1 "thinking that he spoke best to them voted as he wished" (1.145). I do not, however, accept Gomme's simple assertion that Thucydides does not include an opposing speech because "Perikles had the great mass of his fellow citizens behind him" (1956, 1.464). We know only what Thucydides chooses to tell us, and at this point in his narrative he chooses not to tell us about divisions in the city.

13. Cf., e.g., Gomme (1956, 2.175, and the discussion at 2.299 concerning Cleon) and more recently Euben (1990, 178–79).

14. The Corinthian speech of Book 1 (68–71) sets forth the contrast between the active Athenians and the quiet Spartans.

15. See Strauss ([1964] 1978, Chap. 3) on the opposition between Spartan calm and Athenian motion.

16. Gomme (1956, 2.308) agrees with Cleon that there is no indication that divisions existed in Mytilene. Whether they did or did not is beside the point. That Cleon views the city as a unified whole is my point.

17. See how Thucydides fails to give Cleon recognition for the way in which he handles the situation at Sphateria, i.e., Cleon knows what he is doing, but Thucydides constructs the story of that particular campaign to diminish the recognition he deserves.

18. See Orwin (1984) for a full discussion of the debate from this perspective.

19. See Thucydides' analysis of Athens' foreign policy following the death of Pericles which neatly parallels that offered by Pericles himself (2.65).

Chapter Four: Plato

1. Behind this question is the assumption that there is a profound difference between the political philosopher who rules in the city of the *Republic* and the inquisitive philosopher in the person of Socrates who presents himself before the city in the *Apology* and numerous other dialogues. See especially Nichols (1984).

2. Monoson (1994) explores how the theme of *parrhēsia* (freedom of speech) is key for both philosophy and democracy at Athens, thus similarly relating these philosophic and democratic practices that share certain key elements.

3. Euben (1990, chap. 6), drawing on Nussbaum (1986), reads tragedy as a model for democracy. Insofar as he also reads the dialogue form as dependent on tragedy, he draws into his analysis the democratic principles which I also explore, though he adds certain qualifications (e.g., p. 275). See especially pp. 265–66 and 273 where he develops his claims about the "community" that exists at Cephalus' house and its relation to the community created in the speech of the *Republic*.

4. As with every chapter in this volume, a disclaimer is in order: I deal here only with two dialogues. Other dialogues are as important, especially the discussions of democracy in the *Politicus* and the *Laws*. Time and space are limiting, but much more needs to be done on this topic, particularly with regard to these two dialogues.

5. See here Thucydides' discussion of how the Athenians were driven to set sail for Sicily by eros (6.24), and recall Pericles' plea to the Athenians to be lovers of Athens.

6. Aristophanes' wonderful comedy *The Birds* shows the same movement. Two men go off to the land of the birds to found the natural city, one that will satisfy their pleasures and be open to all. At first they welcome all comers to their utopia, but by the end of the comedy the doors must be closed and the hope of complete openness yields to the careful scrutiny of each potential citizen.

7. There is considerable speculation that Alcibiades was spending the time before coming to Agathon's house disfiguring the Hermae, an action that has dire consequences for the execution of the Athenian expedition to Sicily. See Thucydides 6.28–29.

8. We are told by Aristodemus that Eryximachus and his young lover Phaedrus, along with other identified guests, departed for home (223b–c).

9. On the use of the lot in jury trials and of the machines devised to provide for a random assignment of jurors and cases, see, for example, Aristotle's *Athenian Constitution* 63–66. The machines were to help avoid corruption (64.2), but we have no idea how successful they were. In Callipolis, admittedly, the lots are to be manipulated so that the *phaulos* blames chance rather than the rulers for each mating with a less than most desirable mate (460a).

10. Aristotle's *Athenian Constitution* 24.3, 27.2–4, and commentary in Rhodes ([1981] 1993).

11. Cf. Euben's similar reflections on this scene (1990, 245–46).

Chapter Five: Aristotle

1. I shall discuss democracy only as it appears in the *Politics*. I do not address whether Aristotle wrote the *Athenian Constitution* or whether

that is the product of one of his students, nor do I address whether the categories of democracy in the *Politics* influenced the writing of Athenian history in the *Athenian Constitution*.

2. See Saxonhouse (1985, chap. 4) for a discussion of what I call the "limits of observation" and an elaboration of this point with regard to both slaves and women. See also Nichols (1992, 19–24).

3. Aristotle, of course, does not turn to gender or blond hair, and I introduce them only so that we keep in mind the universality of his analysis and its application far beyond ancient Athens.

4. For further discussion of this section, see Saxonhouse (1982) and Dobbs (1985).

5. Aristotle repeats this point about what we call a regime in which the minority are poor and the majority are rich in Book 4, Chapter 4.

6. I use both the male and the female pronoun here. I am not consistent in this usage for the discussion of Aristotle, but I try to use both when discussing general principles and the male pronoun when referring specifically to Aristotelian expectations. Aristotle on women is a complicated issue. I do not go so far as to argue that he wishes to include them in political life, as does Levy (1990), but see my more detailed discussion in Saxonhouse (1985, chap. 4).

7. See above, chapter 1, section V, pp. 25–27.

8. The word *kurion* is difficult to translate; often it is translated as "superior to" as in the "male is superior to the female"; I prefer and find more consistent the translation "has authority over." See my discussion of this word in Saxonhouse (1985, 74).

9. I see this as the central and perhaps most important chapter in Aristotle's *Politics*. It is a chapter certainly reminiscent of Thrasymachus' argument in the first book of the *Republic*.

10. Davis comes to a somewhat similar conclusion by a different route. Considering the differences between "what is" and what "ought to be," he concludes, "If every regime depends on what the city is thought to be, said to be or called, then every regime is in some sense democratic. . . . Political rule requires some measure of consent and is to this extent democratic" (n.d. 10–12).

11. See further Nichols (1992) for a full discussion of this aspect of the *Politics*.

12. For instance, at one point in his article Wolin claims: "'[C]on-stitutional democracy' is not a seamless web of two complementary notions but an ideological construction designed not to realize democracy but to reconstitute it and, as a consequence, repress it" (1994, 32).

13. While Aristotle claims that decrees have no greater legitimacy than the force of numbers in the assembly, he appears to assume that "history" or "antiquity" gives a legitimacy to law not based on force. This, it seems to me, is a place where Aristotle's analysis could be questioned.

14. This qualification applies, we should note, to oligarchies as well if the officers and not the *nomoi* rule.

15. Cf. Yack who, relying on the work of Robin Osborne (1985), writes concerning 1292b25 and 1318b–19a, where Aristotle argues for an agrarian democracy as the best form of democracy: "Athenian democracy as actually practiced corresponds much better to this model of agrarian democracy than to the urban-based mob rule with which it is usually identified.

"Many modern readers mistakenly think of Athens as a city dominated by its urban mass. As a result, most readers assume that Aristotle has Athens in mind when he describes the . . . worst form of democracy (*Pol.* 1292a, 1293a). But Aristotle himself never explicitly identifies Athens with his worst form of democracy" (Yack 1993, 75).

16. At the beginning of Book 4, of course, he had identified oligarchy as the "opposite" of democracy, just as the north and south winds are opposites. See above, p. 131.

17. Aristotle certainly does not go this far, but his study of slavery, where he finds that the slave does not necessarily give birth to the slave (1255b1–4) nor the good man to the good son, suggests perhaps that inherited wealth may say nothing about the abilities of an individual beyond that he or she is favored by chance.

18. The word used here, *prophasis*, is the same word used by Thucydides when he describes the "excuses" that Athens and Lacedaemonia use when they are trying to justify the resort to military force against one another (e.g., 1.23 and 1.126). The implication of Thucydides is that these *prophaseis* are used to cover up the real reasons for the outbreak of the war. Barker (1946, 186) gives a quite powerful translation

of Aristotle's sentence: "The devices adopted in constitutions for fobbing the masses off with sham rights are five in number."

19. The democratic theorists of the 1960s who praised the stabilizing, positive effects of apathy surprisingly seem to have a strong ally in Aristotle. See above, chapter 1, section V, pp. 25–26.

Bibliography

Arendt, Hannah. [1954] 1977. "Tradition and the Modern Age." In *Between Past and Future*. New York: Penguin Books.

Arendt, Hannah. 1958. *The Human Condition*. Chicago: University of Chicago Press.

Arendt, Hannah. 1963. *On Revolution*. New York: The Viking Press.

Bain, Alexander. 1873. *The Minor Works of George Grote: With Critical Remarks on His Intellectual Character, Writings, and Speeches*. London: John Murray.

Barker, Ernest, translation with introduction, notes, and appendices. 1946. *The Politics*, by Aristotle. Oxford: Oxford University Press.

Beiner, Ronald. 1990. "Hannah Arendt and Leo Strauss: The Uncommenced Dialogue." *Political Theory* 18:238–54.

Benardete, Seth. 1969. *Herodotean Inquiries*. The Hague: Martinus Nijhoff.

Bloom, Allan, translation with notes and an interpretive essay. 1968. *The Republic*, by Plato. New York: Basic Books.

Booras, Harris J. 1934. *Hellenic Independence and America's Contribution to the Cause*. Ruthland, Vt.: Tuttle.

Carter, L. B. 1986. *The Quiet Athenian*. Oxford: Clarendon Press.

Cline, Myrtle A. 1930. *American Attitude Toward the Greek War of Independence, 1821–1828*. Atlanta: Higgins McArthur.

Collingwood, R. G. 1939. *An Autobiography*. Oxford: Oxford University Press.

Connor, W. R. 1971. *The New Politicians of the Fifth-Century*. Princeton: Princeton University Press.

Constant, Benjamin. [1819] 1988. "The Liberty of the Ancients Compared with That of the Moderns." In *Political Writings*. Translated and edited by Biancamaria Fontana. Cambridge: Cambridge University Press.

Dahl, Robert. 1989. *Democracy and Its Critics*. New Haven: Yale University Press.

Dakin, Douglas. 1955. *British and American Philhellenes during the War of Greek Independence, 1829–1833*. Thessaloniki: Hetaireia Makedonikon Spoudon.

Davis, Michael. n.d. "Judging the Judge: Political Philosophy in *Politics* III." Manuscript.

Demand, Nancy. 1988. "Herodotus and Metoikesis in the Persian Wars." *American Journal of Philology* 109:416–23.

de Ste. Croix, G. E. M. 1981. *The Class Struggle in the Ancient Greek World from the Archaic Age to the Arab Conquests*. Ithaca, N.Y.: Cornell University Press.

Dobbs, Darrell. 1985. "Aristotle's Anticommunism." *American Journal of Political Science* 29:29–46.

Dossa, Shiraz. 1989. *The Public Realm and the Public Self: The Political Theory of Hannah Arendt*. Waterloo, Ontario: Wilfrid Laurier University Press.

Ehrenberg, Victor. 1950. "The Origins of Democracy." *Historia* 1:515–48.

Euben, J. Peter. 1978. "Political Equality and the Greek Polis." In *Liberalism and the Modern Polity: Essays in Contemporary Political Theory*, edited by Michael J. Gargas McGrath. New York: Marcel Dekker.

Euben, J. Peter. 1990. *The Tragedy of Political Theory: The Road Not Taken*. Princeton: Princeton University Press.

Farrar, Cynthia. 1988. *The Origins of Democratic Thinking: The Invention of Politics in Classical Athens*. Cambridge: Cambridge University Press.

Finley, M. I. 1973. *Democracy: Ancient and Modern*. New Brunswick, N.J.: Rutgers University Press.

Finley, M. I. 1981. "Politics and Political Theory." In *The Legacy of Greece: A New Appraisal*, edited by M. I. Finley. Oxford: Clarendon Press.

Flory, Stewart, 1987. *The Archaic Smile of Herodotus*. Detroit: Wayne State University Press.

Fustel de Coulanges, Numa Denis. [1864] 1980. *The Ancient City: A Study on the Religion, Laws, and Institutions of Greece and Rome*. Reprint with a new foreword by Arnaldo Momigliano and S. C. Humphreys. Baltimore: The Johns Hopkins University Press.

Gillies, John. 1831. *The History of Ancient Greece, Its Colonies and Conquests from the Earliest Accounts Till the Division of the Macedonian Empire in the East: Including the History of Literature, Philosophy, and the Fine Arts.* Philadelphia: Thomas Wordle.

Gomme, A. W. 1956. *A Historical Commentary on Thucydides.* Vols. 1–2. Oxford: Clarendon Press.

Grote, George. 1851. *History of Greece.* Third Edition. 12 vols. London: John Murray.

Hall, Edith. 1989. *Inventing the Barbarian: Greek Self-Definition through Tragedy.* Oxford: Clarendon Press.

Hamburger, Joseph. 1965. *Intellectuals in Politics: John Stuart Mill and the Philosophic Radicals.* New Haven: Yale University Press.

Hansen, Mogens Herman. 1983. *The Athenian Ecclesia: A Collection of Articles, 1976–83.* Copenhagen: Museum Tusculanum Press.

Hansen, Mogens Herman. 1989. *Was Athens a Democracy? Popular Rule, Liberty and Equality in Ancient and Modern Political Thought.* Historisk-filosofiske Meddelelser Det Kongelige Danske Videnskabernes Selskab 59. Copenhagen: Commissioner, Munksgaard.

Hansen, Mogens Herman. 1991. *The Athenian Democracy in the Age of Demosthenes: Structure, Principles and Ideology.* Translated by J. A. Crook. Oxford and Cambridge, Mass.: Basil Blackwell.

Hartog, François. 1988. *The Mirror of Herodotus: The Representation of the Other in the Writing of History.* Translated by Janet Lloyd. Berkeley and Los Angeles: University of California Press.

Herodotus. 1942. *The Persian Wars.* Translated by George Rawlinson. With an introduction by R. B. Godolphin. New York: Random House.

Herodotus. [1954] 1972. *The Histories.* Translated by Aubrey de Sélincourt. Harmondsworth, England: Penguin Books.

Herodotus. 1987. *The History.* Translated by David Grene. Chicago: University of Chicago Press.

Hobbes, Thomas. 1975. *Thucydides.* Edited by Richard Schlatter. New Brunswick, N.J.: Rutgers University Press.

How, W. W., and J. Wells. [1912] 1989. *A Commentary on Herodotus.* Paperback edition. 2 vols. Oxford: Oxford University Press.

Jones, A. H. M. [1957] 1964. *Athenian Democracy*. Oxford: Basil Blackwell & Mott.

Kagan, Donald. 1965. *The Great Dialogue: History of Greek Political Thought from Homer to Polybius*. New York: The Free Press; London: Collier-Macmillan.

Kagan, Donald. 1991. *Pericles of Athens and the Birth of Democracy*. New York: The Free Press; Toronto: Collier-Macmillan.

Klein, Jacob. 1965. *A Commentary on Plato's "Meno."* Chapel Hill: University of North Carolina Press.

Klein, Jacob. 1977. "The Political Thought of Plato and Aristotle." Paper presented at the annual meeting of the American Political Science Association, Washington, D.C.

Levy, Harold L. 1990. "Does Aristotle Exclude Women from Politics?" *Review of Politics* 52:397–416.

Long, Orie William. [1935] 1963. *Literary Pioneers: Early American Explorers of European Culture*. Reissued, New York: Russell and Russell.

Manville, Philip B. 1990. *The Origins of Citizenship in Ancient Athens*. Princeton: Princeton University Press.

Miles, Edwin. 1974. "The Young American Nation and the Classical World." *Journal of the History of Ideas* 35:259–74.

Mill, John Stuart. 1846. "Grote's History of Greece [1]." In *Collected Works of John Stuart Mill*. Edited by J. M. Robson. Vol. 24, *Newspaper Writings: January 1835–June 1847*, edited by Ann P. Robson and J. M. Robson. Toronto: University of Toronto Press; London: Routledge and Kegan Paul, 1986. [Originally published in *Spectator*, 4 April 1846, pp. 327–28.]

Mill, John Stuart. 1847. "Grote's History of Greece [2]." In *Collected Works of John Stuart Mill*. Edited by J. M. Robson. Vol. 24, *Newspaper Writings: January 1835–June 1847*, edited by Ann P. Robson and J. M. Robson. Toronto: University of Toronto Press; London: Routledge and Kegan Paul, 1986. [Originally published in *Spectator*, 5 June 1847, pp. 543–44.]

Mill, John Stuart. 1849. "Grote's History of Greece [3]." In *Collected Works of John Stuart Mill*. Edited by J. M. Robson. Vol. 25, *Newspaper Writings: December 1847–July 1873*, edited by Ann P. Robson and J. M. Robson. Toronto: University of Toronto Press; London: Routledge and Kegan Paul, 1986. [Originally published in *Spectator*, 3 March, 1849, pp. 202–3.]

Mitford, William. 1838. *The History of Greece.* 8 vols. Revised by William King, editor of the first posthumous edition. London: T. Cadell, Strand, and W. Blackwood and Sons, Edinburgh.

Momigliano, Arnaldo. 1952. *George Grote and the Study of Greek History.* London: H. K. Lewis.

Momigliano, Arnoldo. 1979. "Persian Empire and Greek Freedom." In *The Idea of Freedom: Essays in Honor of Isaiah Berlin.* Edited by Alan Ryan. Oxford: Oxford University Press.

Monoson, Sarah. 1994. "Frank Speech, Democracy, and Philosophy: Plato's Debt to a Democratic Strategy of Civic Discourse." In *Athenian Political Thought and the Reconstruction of American Democracy,* edited by J. Peter Euben, John R. Wallach, and Josiah Ober. Ithaca, N.Y.: Cornell University Press.

Mulgan, Richard. 1984. "Liberty in Ancient Greece." In *Conceptions of Liberty in Political Philosophy,* edited by Zbigniew Pelczynski and John Gray. New York: St. Martin's Press.

Nichols, Mary P. 1984. "The Republic's Two Alternatives: Philosopher-Kings and Socrates." *Political Theory* 12:252–74.

Nichols, Mary P. 1992. *Citizens and Statesmen: A Study of Aristotle's Politics.* Savage, Md.: Rowman and Littlefield.

Nussbaum, Martha C. 1986. *The Fragility of Goodness: Luck and Ethics in Greek Tragedy and Philosophy.* Cambridge: Cambridge University Press.

Ober, Josiah. 1989a. *Mass and Elite in Democratic Athens.* Princeton: Princeton University Press.

Ober, Josiah. 1989b. "The Nature of Athenian Democracy." Review of *The Athenian Assembly in the Age of Demosthenes,* by M. H. Hansen. *Classical Philology* 84:322–34.

Ober, Josiah. 1993. "Thucydides' Criticism of Democratic Knowledge." In *Nomodeiktes: Greek Studies in Honor of Martin Ostwald,* edited by Ralph M. Rosen and Joseph Farrell. Ann Arbor: University of Michigan Press.

Orwin, Clifford. 1984. "The Just and the Advantageous in Thucydides: The Case of the Mytilenian Debate." *American Political Science Review* 78:485–94.

Osborne, Robin. 1985. *Demos: The Discovery of Classical Attika.* Cambridge: Cambridge University Press.

Ostwald, Martin. 1986. *From Popular Sovereignty to the Sovereignty of Law: Law, Society and Politics in Fifth-Century Athens.* Berkeley and Los Angeles: University of California Press.

Paine, Thomas. 1989. *Political Writings.* Edited by Bruce Kuklick. Cambridge: Cambridge University Press.

Palmer, R. R. 1953. "Notes on the Use of the Word 'Democracy'." *Political Science Quarterly* 68:203–26.

Pangle, Thomas. 1988. *The Spirit of Modern Republicanism: The Moral Vision of the American Founders and the Philosophy of Locke.* Chicago: University of Chicago Press.

Pappas, Paul Constantine. 1985. *The United States and the Greek War for Independence.* Boulder: East European Monographs, no. 173. New York: Columbia University Press.

Podlecki, Anthony J. 1986. "*Polis* and Monarch in Early Attic Tragedy." In *Greek Tragedy and Political Theory,* edited by J. Peter Euben, 76–100. Berkeley and Los Angeles: University of California Press.

Reinhold, Meyer. 1984. *Classica Americana: The Greek and Roman Heritage in the United States.* Detroit: Wayne State University Press.

Rhodes, P. J. 1972. *The Athenian Boule.* Oxford: Clarendon Press.

Rhodes, P. J. [1981] 1993. *A Commentary on Aristotle's "Athenaion Politeia."* First published, Oxford: Clarendon Press; Paperback edition, Oxford: Oxford University Press.

Richard, Carl J. 1994. *The Founders and the Classics: Greece, Rome, and the American Enlightenment.* Cambridge: Harvard University Press.

Roberts, Jennifer Tolbert. 1994. *Athens on Trial: The Antidemocratic Tradition in Western Thought.* Princeton: Princeton University Press.

Saxonhouse, Arlene W. 1982. "Family, Polity, and Unity: Aristotle on Socrates' Community of Wives." *Polity* 15:202–19.

Saxonhouse, Arlene W. 1983. "An Unspoken Theme in Plato's *Gorgias*: War." *Interpretation* 11:139–69.

Saxonhouse, Arlene W. 1985. *Women in the History of Political Thought: Ancient Greece to Machiavelli.* Westport, Conn.: Praeger.

Saxonhouse, Arlene W. 1992. *Fear of Diversity: The Birth of Political Science in Ancient Greek Thought.* Chicago: University of Chicago Press.

Sealey, Raphael. 1974. "The Origins of *Demokratia.*" *California Studies in Classical Antiquity,* 6:252–95. Berkeley and Los Angeles: University of California Press.

Sealey, Raphael. 1987. *The Athenian Republic: Democracy or the Rule of Law?* University Park: Pennsylvania State University Press.

Sinclair, R.K. 1988. *Democracy and Participation in Athens.* Cambridge: Cambridge University Press.

Stanyan, Temple. 1751. *The Grecian History.* 2 vols. London: Printed for J. and R. Tonson and S. Draper in the Strand.

Stockton, David. 1990. *The Classical Athenian Democracy.* Oxford: Oxford University Press.

Stone, I.F. 1988. *The Trial of Socrates.* Boston: Little, Brown.

Strauss, Barry S. 1986. *Athens after the Peloponnesian War: Class, Faction and Policy, 403–386 B.C.* Ithaca, N.Y.: Cornell University Press.

Strauss, Leo. [1964] 1978. *The City and Man.* Phoenix edition. Chicago: University of Chicago Press.

Thucydides. 1954. *The Peloponnesian War.* Translated by Rex Warner. Harmondsworth, England: Penguin Books.

Thucydides. 1982. *The Peloponnesian War.* Translated by Richard Crawley. New York: Random House.

Turner, Frank M. 1981. *The Greek Heritage in Victorian Britain.* New Haven: Yale University Press.

Vernant, Jean-Pierre. 1982. *The Origins of Greek Thought.* Translated from the French. Ithaca, N.Y.: Cornell University Press.

Vlastos, Gregory. 1953. "*Isonomia.*" *American Journal of Philology* 74: 337–66.

Webster, Daniel. 1903. *The Writings and Speeches of Daniel Webster.* 18 vols. Boston: Little, Brown.

Whitehead, David. 1986. *The Demes of Attica 508/7–ca. 250B.C.: A Political & Social Study.* Princeton: Princeton University Press.

Wills, Garry. 1992. *Lincoln at Gettysburg: The Words that Remade America.* New York: Simon and Schuster.

Wolin, Sheldon. 1994. "Norm and Form: The Constitutionalizing of Democracy." In *Athenian Political Thought and the Reconstruction of American Democracy,* edited by J. Peter Euben, John R. Wallach, and Josiah Ober. Ithaca, N.Y.: Cornell University Press.

Wood, Ellen Meiksins. 1988. *Peasant-Citizen and Slave: The Foundations of Athenian Democracy*. London: Verso.

Wood, Ellen Meiksins, and Neal Wood. 1978. *Class Ideology and Ancient Political Theory: Socrates, Plato, and Aristotle in Social Context*. Oxford: Basil Blackwell; New York: Oxford University Press.

Yack, Bernard. 1993. *The Problem of a Political Animal: Community, Justice, and Conflict in Aristotelian Political Thought*. Berkeley and Los Angeles: University of California Press.

Zimmern, Alfred. [1911] 1922. *The Greek Commonwealth: Politics and Economics in Fifth-Century Athens*. Third Edition, rev. Oxford: Clarendon Press.

Index

Aristotle (*cont.*)
133–34, 136–39; on political stability, 130, 135–38, 140; on polity, 122–23, 131, 135–36; on *psēphisma*, 128, 131, 133, 157n.13; on rule of the best, 129, 135; on rule of law, 131–32; on slavery, 118–19, 157n.17; on Socrates' city (Callipolis), 120; on tension between justice and nature, 146; typologies in, 115, 122–23, 135. Works: *Athenian Constitution*, 4, 155nn.9, 1; *Politics*, 115–41

assembly (*ecclēsia*), 140; absence in Aristotle's definition of the citizen, 126; absence in Callipolis, 100, 111; Aristotle on, 130, 132–34, 139–40; Athenagoras on, 82; attendance at, 5; language of in Plato's dialogues, 95, 100, 107; in Thucydides, analyses of, 70–71, 75, 78–79, 85, 144–45

Assyrians, 39, 45
Athenagoras (Syracusan leader), 82–83, 85
Athenian Constitution (Aristotle), 4, 155nn.9, 1
Athenian Democracy (A. H. M. Jones), 5
Athens on Trial (Jennifer Tolbert Roberts), 147n.2, 149n.9
Autobiography, An (R. G. Collingwood), 10

Babylonia, customs of, 40–43, 48, 57, 151n.11
Bain, Alexander, 21
Barker, Ernest, 157n.18
Beiner, Ronald, 149n.15
Benardete, Seth, 51, 151nn.6, 11, 152n.15
Berelson, Bernard, 26
Birds (Aristophanes), 155n.6
boulē (council), 108, 148n.4
Burke, Edmund, 13

Callipolis, 60, 85, 99–101, 153n.6; compared to Athens, 104; compared to Socrates' democracy, 110–11; lot in, 155n.9
Cambyses (Persian king), 49–50
Carter, L. B., 6, 148n.4
Cephalus, 99
Cicero, Marcus Tullius, 151n.7
citizen, 34, 105–06, 111, 126; Arendt on, 23–25; in Athens, 5–6, 27, 101, 105, 108; Cleon on, 74–75; definition of in Aristotle, 125–30, 140–41; Diodotus on, 76–77; and equality, 41–42, 121; identification of, 93, 109; and *isonomia*, 33; in Pericles' speeches, 60, 62–63, 66–71, 105
City and Man, The (Leo Strauss), 110
Cleisthenes, 32–33, 37–38, 51
Cleomenes (Spartan king), 55
Cleon, 72, 80; on *dēmokratia*, 73; on justice, 75–76; parallels to Pericles, 73–75, 78; speech, 72–75; Thucydides' attitude towards, 75, 154n.17
Collingwood, R. G., 10
communal decision-making, 72, 76, 79, 83–84, 132
compulsion: absence in Socrates' definition of democracy, 108; in democratic Athens, 109; in *Symposium*, 94–95, 97
Connor, W. R., 4
Constant, Benjamin, 27
constructed equality, 24, 34, 122, 144
Crawley, Richard, 147n.2
Creon, 8
Cyclops, 123, 141
Cyrus, 39–40, 53

Dahl, Robert, 26, 148n.2
Darius: becomes King of Persia, 56; defender of monarchy, 53–55
Davis, Michael, 156n.10

Grene, David, 36, 47
Grote, George, *History of Greece*, 18–21, 38

Haemon, 8
Hall, Edith, 151n.12
Hamilton, Alexander, 12–13
Hansen, M. H., 5, 6, 147n.2, 150n.2
Harmodius, song of, 42
Hastings, battle of, 21
Hephaestus (Egyptian priest), 39, 48
Hermocrates (Syracusan leader), 81–83, 86
Herodotus, 1, 29, 34–57, 86, 117–18, 143–44, 147n.1; on customs of the Babylonians, 40–43, 46; debate among Persian conspirators, 49–56; on defects of democracy, 55; on equality, 32–36, 40–49, 51–52, 53, 56–57, 144; on the free Greeks, 35, 37, 38, 51; on freedom and democracy, 37–39, 50, 53–54, 57; as historian, 36–37
hierarchy, 49; Aristotle on, 118–20, 129; in Pericles' Funeral Oration, 63, 153n.5
Hipparchus, 39, 42
Hippias, 39, 42
Histaeus (Herodotean character), 152n.14
History of Ancient Greece (John Gillies), 17
History of Greece (George Grote), 20
Hobbes, Thomas, 15; on Thucydides, 2–3, 59, 86, 144; translation of Thucydides, 3, 148n.3
Homer, 23
How, W. W., 38, 151n.13
hupeuthunon (accounting), 50

isēgoria (equal opportunity to speak), 33, 36, 55, 57; defended by Diodotus, 77, 80

isokratia (equality of power), 34
isonomia (equality before/within the law), 36, 42, 57, 101, 144; Otanes on, 50, 53, 54; in Socrates' description of democracy, 104; as synonym for democracy, 32–33, 35, 150nn.2, 3; Vlastos on, 41

Jackson, Andrew, 14
Jones, A. H. M., 5, 7, 57
Jones, Morris, 26

Kagan, Donald, 1, 37–38, 50–51, 54
kingship, 45, 54, 56, 115, 129. *See also* monarchy
Klein, Jacob, 115–16
kurion (authority), 156n.8

Lacedaemonia (see Sparta)
Latin, 14
Lipset, Seymour Martin, 26
logos (reason, speech), in the definition of Aristotle's citizen, 124–26, 129, 136, 141, 145
lot, 52, 101, 104, 107, 108, 136, 155n.9
love: in Pericles' Funeral Oration, 9; Socrates as expert, 94; in *Symposium*, 91. *See also* eros

Madison, James, 13
Maeandrius (ruler of Samos), 35, 50
Manville, Philip, 93
Marathon, battle of, 21
Medes, 39–40, 45
Megabyzus (Persian conspirator), 52, 54–56
Miles, Edwin, 149n.10
Mill, James, 19
Mill, John Stuart, 18–21
Mitford, William, 1, 17–21
mob, 1, 13, 18, 22; Megabyzus on, 52; in Plato's *Symposium*, 92, 94, 97–98

tyranny, 97; relation to democracy in Aristotle, 127, 132–35, 136, 138; as successor to democracy in Plato, 90, 94, 98, 103, 110–13

Vernant, J. P., 152n.4
Vlastos, Gregory, 33, 41, 42, 150nn.2, 3, 152n.15

Warner, Rex, 3–4, 148n.2
Waterville, Michigan, 12
Webster, Daniel, 15
Wells, J., 38, 151n.13
Whitehead, David, 148n.4
Wills, Garry, 149n.10

Wolin, Sheldon, 132, 157n.12
Wood, Ellen, 148n.5
Wood, Ellen and Neal, 87, 112, 134
Woodruff, Benjamin, 11

Xenophon, 94
Xerxes, 44

Yack, Bernard, 157n.15
Ypsilanti, Demetrius, 11
Ypsilanti, Michigan, 11

Zeus, 8–9
Zimmern, Alfred, *The Greek Commonwealth*, 21

DATE DUE